176 Ways to
INVOLVE
PARENTS

Practical Strategies for Partnering With Families

Betty Boult

CORWIN PRESS
A SAGE Publications Company
Thousand Oaks, California

For information:

Corwin Press, Inc.
A Sage Publications Company
2455 Teller Road
Thousand Oaks, California 91320
www.corwinpress.com

Sage Publications Ltd.
1 Oliver's Yard
55 City Road
London EC1Y 1SP
United Kingdom

Sage Publications India Pvt. Ltd.
B-42, Panchsheel Enclave
Post Box 4109
New Delhi 110 017 India

Printed in the United States of America.

This book is printed on acid-free paper.

Library of Congress Cataloging-in-Publication Data

Boult, Betty.
176 ways to involve parents: Practical strategies for partnering with families / Betty Boult.— 2nd ed.
  p. cm.
Includes bibliographical references and index.
ISBN 1-4129-3668-3 (cloth) — ISBN 1-4129-3669-1 (pbk.)
  1. Education—Parent participation. 2. Home and school. I. Title:
One hundred seventy-six ways to involve parents. II. Title.
LB1048.5.B68 2006
371.19'2—dc22   2005037814

06 07 08 09 10 10 9 8 7 6 5 4 3 2 1

Acquisitions Editor:	Cathy Hernandez
Editorial Assistant:	Charline Wu
Project Editor:	Kate Peterson
Copy Editor:	Mary L. Tederstrom
Typesetter:	C&M Digitals (P) Ltd.
Indexer:	Pamela Van Huss
Cover Designer:	Scott Van Atta

176 Ways to INVOLVE PARENTS

second edition

Contents

Preface

In many schools, parents are welcomed as equal partners in their child's education. Educators at such institutions believe that working in concert with families to provide quality education to students is a necessity, not an option. The partnership of school and home ranges from having parents check their children's homework to actively involving parents as key decision makers in the governance of the schools and the district. Three decades of research on student achievement validates the importance of involving parents as educational partners. Research clearly shows that parents directly impact their children's academic achievement through the discussions they have with and the expectations they set for their children. In examining the impact of parent involvement in the early years and on the achievement of disadvantaged children, Wendy Miedel and Arthur Reynolds (1999) reported that if parents were actively involved in preschool and kindergarten, children in Grade 8 achieved significantly higher in reading, stayed in school longer, and were less likely to be placed in special education programs.

Joyce Epstein and Susan Dauber found that the level of parent involvement is directly related to the practices schools and teachers have in place and does not depend on race, ethnicity, size of the family, marital status, or the education of the parents (as cited in Chen & Chandler, 2001). Clearly, schools need to proactively develop both policies and practices to ensure parents are involved in educating their children both at home and at school (Chen & Chandler, 2001).

It is important to note, however, that even if the opportunity is not offered, many parents will seek the right to be meaningfully involved. Across both the United States and Canada, the role of the parent in the education system has been legitimized by major reforms, which in turn have defined parents' rights. Specifically, recent legislation in many jurisdictions has given parents an increased voice in the governance of the school system at both the school and district levels, established an appeal process for the redress of parent and student grievances, and provided access to records for parents. Increasingly, parents see themselves as active participants in education and are exercising their rights to be involved at every level.

While the relationship between parents and schools may pose new challenges to all involved, the benefits of parent involvement have been proven. They include enhanced student self-esteem, increased academic achievement, and improved communication. Schools strengthen what they do by working collaboratively with parents.

176 Ways to Involve Parents: Practical Strategies for Partnering With Families is a hands-on guide for those who recognize the need and benefit of involving parents and is presented in four parts.

Part 1: *Making It Happen* focuses on ways to convey that by meaningfully involving parents, student learning is strengthened, parents become advocates instead of adversaries, and all partners have a sense of ownership of public education. It provides ideas on how to work with both the students and their families to involve each in the life of their school.

Part 2: *Creating the Climate* contains well-thought-out and practical methods of promoting and supporting communication and change. This section frames a plan for ensuring that the school is inviting to the public. Readers are encouraged to laud their school's successes and programs by marketing education to the community it serves.

Part 3: *Sustaining the Involvement* discusses how to effectively engage parents and the business community in shared ownership of the educational system. Ideas to enrich the quality of school life through encouraging, expecting, and supporting parent and business involvement are offered. Underlying the ideas is the belief that providing education to students is a shared responsibility and all partners must have a role in its delivery.

Part 4: *Venturing Beyond the Bake Sale* provides ample evidence that it is imperative that schools allow for meaningful parent involvement beyond their accepted and traditional role as fundraisers. Strategies for bringing about shared governance at the school and district levels are offered, and the concept of shared ownership of educating children is reinforced.

Each part provides research related to the particular topic being addressed. This introduction reinforces the indisputable case for a partnership with parents. Several "Ideas to Use" are offered for each topic and include practical methods to involve families in the education of their children.

The second edition of *176 Ways to Involve Parents: Practical Strategies for Partnering With Families* has been reorganized for greater clarity and increased usability. It presents expanded and updated references to the research base that supports the strategies. In addition, many strategies have been revised or expanded, and numerous suggestions for working with families in diverse communities have been included.

Publisher's Acknowledgments

Corwin Press gratefully acknowledges the contributions of the following reviewers:

Mary Ann Beckman, Director of Special Education
Arrowhead District Special Education Cooperative,
Hartland, WI

Judy Chapman, District Principal for Curriculum,
Instruction, and Assessment
School District #34, Abbotsford, B.C., Canada

Nic Cooper, Principal
Saline Middle School, Saline, MI

Chris Ferguson, Program Associate
Southwest Educational Development Laboratory,
Austin, TX

Jane E. Hampton, Principal
Oak Mountain Elementary School, Birmingham, AL

Pamela S. Quebodeaux, Principal
Dolby Elementary School, Lake Charles, LA

Christina Ross Daniels, Special Education/Behavior
    Modification Teacher
Picayune Center for Alternative Education, Picayune, MS

Wanda Routier, Associate Lecturer
University of Wisconsin–Milwaukee, Milwaukee, WI

Linda R. Vogel, Assistant Professor of Educational Leadership
    and Policy Studies
University of Northern Colorado, Greeley, CO

About the Author

**Betty Boult**, EdD, is currently an adjunct professor and educational consultant. She retired from the position of assistant superintendent of School District No. 43 (Coquitlam) in British Columbia in June 2000. She has served as director of instruction (curriculum), supervisor of staff development, principal, assistant principal, teacher-librarian, and classroom teacher. Her background experience ranges from primary to adult education in both Canada and the United States. In addition to these full-time positions, she has served as a provincial community education consultant, a guest lecturer for the University of Lethbridge, a sessional instructor for the University of Alberta, and instructor for Nova Southeastern University. She has done part-time consulting with an international consulting company. During the past fifteen years, she has been contracted to do workshops and seminars at the district, provincial, and international levels. In addition, she has appeared on educational television and published numerous articles.

Introduction

For the past thirty-seven years, I have been involved in education in a number of different roles and locations—from classroom teacher to assistant superintendent to adjunct professor. Most recently I have worked with teachers and administrators pursuing their doctoral degrees and site-based administrators seeking district positions. These career experiences have revealed the need for teachers and administrators to determine how to best partner with parents. Educators know that this relationship is integral to good education but are somewhat concerned about how to involve families effectively. They see this both as a challenge and as an opportunity.

At every stage of my career, the topic of parents and their involvement in the system has conjured up a variety of reactions from educators. As a beginning teacher, some of my colleagues told me how much I would enjoy the extra pair of hands, the skills parents brought to the classroom, and the insights parents would share about their children. I was told by other colleagues that parents were to be guarded against, as they were unreasonable and wanted teachers to do everything for their children. Some stated that many parents did not assume responsibility for their children's actions. Above all, I was warned, parents could not be pleased. Many schools I worked in had minimal parent involvement, and in more than one situation, parents were treated as unwelcome intruders. Many staffs worked hard at keeping parents at a distance.

During the course of my career, I became very interested in understanding the dynamics and impact of parent involvement. I believed I would provide quality education to children if I worked closely with parents. The ideas presented in this book have been gleaned from years of working with educators and with parents. I have watched this work improve the quality of education for children by groups not only believing in the partnership but also finding ways to work together.

I would ask the reader to know that when the term *parent* is used throughout the book, it refers to the primary caregiver of the child. The reader may use the word *parent* interchangeably with *family*. Researchers at the North Central Regional Education Laboratory (2005) stated that the terms *parent involvement* and *family involvement* can be used interchangeably. Children may live with one parent, but the role of parent could be assumed by members of the extended family. It is also a cultural matter, as extended families will often have a major role in raising the child.

Society is undergoing an era of greater accountability with tremendous implications for education. It is evident that education must be a collaborative venture between parents and educators. I hope your school can benefit from the ideas in this book as you take up the challenges of partnering with families to continue to offer quality education for children in the twenty-first century.

PART 1

Making It Happen

A common finding by Ann Henderson and Karen Mapp (2002), in their synthesis of the research on parent involvement, was that families have a major influence on their children's achievement in school. The authors found that when schools, families, and community organizations work together to support learning, children not only achieve better academically but also stay in school longer.

The key to parent involvement is demonstrating to parents that the school wants them to be a part of school life. The ways parents can be involved are endless, and the need for their involvement is pressing. All parental involvement is important, whether it is at home supporting their child's academic progress, in the classroom assisting groups of students, or serving through a membership on the advisory council. Schools must value whatever time commitment parents and family members make and recognize that these volunteers want to support their children but are not always clear on how to do this. What we do know is that they want to make a difference. Educators must convey to parents and family members that their involvement is essential to the learning process.

Joyce Epstein, a leading researcher in partnerships between schools and parents, identifies practices that need to be in place to develop effective parent involvement. She states that educators need to establish communication strategies that inform families about not only how their children are progressing but also what is happening in the classroom and in the school. Epstein discusses the need for educators to proactively initiate ways in which families can be involved in the operation of the school. Involvement ranges from helping parents support their children's learning at home to sharing the decision-making process. Epstein also describes the need for educators to work with the community to increase family access to resources (Chen & Chandler, 2001).

In order to successfully implement these practices, Epstein recommends that schools develop a parent involvement plan that ensures (a) sharing information on parenting and child development, (b) focusing on two-way communication, (c) finding ways for parents to volunteer and attend school events, (d) supporting children's home studies, (e) increasing the role parents play in decision making, and (f) finding ways for families to access community resources.

This part suggests some practical strategies to involve the whole family.

Starting the School Year

O ver the last few decades there has been a major shift in family structure. The 1950s *Leave It to Beaver* construct of the traditional family has been replaced by a model where both parents are employed outside the family home. Another dimension of that changed model of families is the redefinition of what a family is in today's world. The *Oxford Dictionary's* (2005) definition of *family* includes members of the household. Many children's primary caregivers are not their biological mother or father, and schools need to welcome the different models of families that exist in their communities.

Gwen Rudney (2005) discusses the fact that there is not one model that defines the successful family. She describes two-parent families (most of which are dual-career families), single-parent families, stepparents, blended families, gay parents, economically disadvantaged parents, as well as parents from different cultures. She concludes that there is not a one-size-fits-all family model.

It is the educator's responsibility to accept and work with all types of families. To do this, create an atmosphere that reflects the message that the family and the school need to work together. Offering opportunities where everyone can be involved in a nonthreatening and supportive environment creates a culture of support and a sense of community.

All of these activities need coordination and planning. Divide the tasks up so there is shared responsibility between staff members, the advisory council, and where appropriate, members of the student body.

In this book, the term *advisory council*—defined as a group of people who are working together to improve the quality of school life—will be used in various scenarios encouraging community participation. There are many formal definitions of this term, and in many cases there are legislated expectations involving parent involvement from federal, state, and provincial levels. Many of the Web sites suggested in the index will provide you with these formal definitions. Suffice it to say here that, whether it is the Parent-Teacher Association (PTA), the Home and School Association, the Parent Council, or any other group that has come together, their focus needs to be on improving the quality of school life for the children in that school and district. Recently, when I typed in the words *Parent Advisory Councils* in an Internet search engine to compile a general definition, the search generated 1,180,000 hits.

For example, here is a definition from Nova Scotia (Strait School Board, 2005, para. 2):

> A school advisory council is a legally recognized body composed of the principal and representatives of parents, students, teachers, support staff, and community members who work together to enhance the quality of education provided by the school.
>
> The fundamental purpose of the school advisory council is to ensure that all students receive the best possible learning opportunities by engaging all partners in an ongoing process of shared decision making related to student learning. The primary responsibility of the council is to develop and to implement a school improvement plan in collaboration with school staff.

IDEAS TO USE

1 Begin the school year with a celebration of families.

Convert your traditional September parent-teacher meeting into an evening where the whole family is invited. Include any event or activity that helps parents understand the importance of the family relationship with the school. Consider hosting a barbecue or organizing a flea market. Make sure to have a sign-up booth for school volunteers.

Take this opportunity to determine if there is an interest in establishing or extending support groups for families with specific interests. For example, you could initiate groups for children with special needs, families new to the community, single-parent families, and families learning the English language. The list goes on and should be reflective of your school community needs. This is a win-win opportunity, as you will learn more about your families and community as you support the whole family.

The school does not always have to be the primary initiator of family support groups but can link with many inter-agencies in the community to enhance and increase support.

2 Prepare a welcome package to distribute to new families.

Include business promotions (discounts on pizza or dry cleaning provided by local merchants), maps of the school and town, and folders and pencils imprinted with the school name and logo. Sample newsletters, e-mail addresses, school and district Web site addresses, as well as the names of advisory council members should be included to make parents aware of how the school communicates with its families. Include a list of suggested ways families can be involved in the life of the school as well. Make sure the list is also handed out at registration.

Advertise that the welcome packages are available in a link on your school Web site. Include links to local businesses, restaurants, the chamber of commerce, and other community associations.

Involve students, where appropriate, in preparing these welcome packages.

3 Ensure understanding.

Translate the information into the main languages that are represented in your school community. Either ask parents of that culture to do the translation, or ask them to proof the documents before they are sent home. As part of this activity, use the parents who are core to the operation of the school and have been involved to help plan and develop the package. Parents know what information is helpful to families as they arrive in a new school and/or a new community setting.

4 Offer home visits.

Ask parents if they are interested in having one or more volunteers from the school community drop in to visit them at home. The advisory council can organize and train a group of parents who are interested in helping new families. The visiting parents should discuss community and school resources. Make sure that the volunteers share the same language or culture as the family they are calling on, as it will promote greater communication, comfort, and inclusion.

If possible, have educators involved in these home visits. Teachers may or may not have the time to do this, but if they do, it will further their understanding of the child's behavior in the classroom, as they will have a home context for the children and their families.

5 Survey families at the beginning of the year to identify their expertise.

Use surveys to find out more about families' interests, hobbies, travels, and jobs. Because it is important to collect as many surveys as possible, develop a simple survey that is uncluttered and includes a few items, provides simple directions, and encourages easy responses (Charles & Mertler, 2002). Stress the value of completing the survey in terms of planning for curriculum support and inclusion of family members in school activities.

Consider making the development of the survey part of the social studies or art curriculum depending on the grade levels of your school. Secondary school leadership classes could assume responsibility for the design and implementation of this strategy.

Use online surveys and offer the survey in a number of languages. This could be very helpful, as many families are already receiving large volumes of paperwork at the start of the school year.

Ask parents to share their experiences with the school either at career day programs or as curriculum resource speakers.

Supporting the Whole Family

This classic comment by Joyce Epstein (1995) relates to family involvement. She noted:

> The way schools care about children is reflected in the way schools care about the children's families. If educators view children simply as students, they are likely to see the family as separate from the school. . . . Partners recognize their shared interests in and responsibilities for children, and they work together to create better programs and opportunities for students. (p. 703)

Events that are focused on building the concept of family create opportunities to develop positive relations among the entire school community. The involvement of parents, students, community members, and organizations provides the opportunity for educators to relate to students as whole persons with lives outside of school. Therefore, helping the family helps the student.

IDEAS TO USE

6 Find other ways.

Some families may be reluctant to share personal information with staff. Find other ways to communicate this information.

For example, if parents in the school community attend church services regularly, consider parent information meetings that are held with the support and assistance of community church leaders to deal with any socioeconomic barriers that impede the development of positive teacher-parent relationships.

Encourage cooperation between the partner groups (which could include police, social service agencies, staff, parents, and students) in planning, implementing, and evaluating events. Make sure to plan them well enough in advance so that they can be included in the annual school calendar as well as other community calendars. When creating these opportunities, consult with families as well.

7 Sponsor a family goods exchange.

Recycle goods in this environmentally friendly project. Part of the success of such an event is to ensure that families see the swap meet as an opportunity for all to benefit. Make the swap meet an annual tradition that is linked to other school events such as book fairs, parent-teacher interviews, curriculum updates, or even the kickoff event to the basketball season. By setting the date in the school calendar you can make this a part of the student/parent advisory council fundraising. Charge a nominal fee to rent the tables.

Encourage families to bring items such as skates, skis, winter boots, and parkas as well as children's clothing and toys.

8 Offer English as a Second Language (ESL) classes to parents and others in the community.

Although this comes under the purview of adult teaching centers, find a way to support these classes by working with your local community college and local agencies.

Post the opportunities in the school newsletter and on the school Web site for best results.

9 Provide coping with grief sessions for students and their families.

Too many young persons today suffer from having lost loved ones to violence. Families need support in dealing with depression brought on by unresolved or unaddressed grief issues. School social workers and psychologists can help organize the sessions.

Post contact numbers of important agencies in the welcome package, on the parent handout, and on the district and school Web site.

10 Foster a support group for single parents.

Create opportunities for single parents to meet. Offer parenting sessions combined with social activities. Set it up so that the group meets at the school. Offer in-kind contributions for the group by advertising their meetings and allowing facilitators the use of the photocopier and other office machines. Determine if the parent advisory council will support student baby-sitting for these sessions.

Check with district policy about the use of machines in schools.

11 Facilitate family get-togethers.

Build these family events into the school and parent advisory calendars starting with the September event. To encourage participation, link the social event to a school purpose. For an example, at a secondary school, combine a school picnic with a band fundraising activity.

This strategy can be particularly helpful to language or cultural minority parents. Because language minority students are less likely to participate in sports and other extracurricular activities, their parents are afforded fewer opportunities for interaction with other parents.

Offer school facilities for a parent wine and cheese night, pancake breakfast, car rally, or other social-based activities.

Creating Safe Havens for Students

Appropriate attention to discipline and order helps schools and parents provide a safe environment for students. However, when school is not in session and parents are at work, unattended or improperly supervised young people can present a risk to themselves and their community. Therefore, coalitions must be built to provide for the safety of students during the school day and beyond.

Collaborative efforts between the school, parents, and community can help ensure that students are safely and productively involved on days when not in school. Consequently, connections are forged or strengthened between the home, school, and community.

Volunteers should provide criminal record checks. This is a critical process and is a necessary step to facilitate the safety of students. In cases where volunteers cannot afford to pay for it, the school could fund the process.

IDEAS TO USE

12 Reach out to establishments in the community (such as ice and roller rinks, movie theaters, bowling alleys, and community libraries) that cater to student interests.

Find out if they are willing to donate space or develop programs during the school's noninstructional days. Ask the businesses what community service the students could offer in return.

This is a viable organizational task for the parent advisory council in collaboration with a student advisory council/leadership program at a middle or secondary school.

13 Offer recreational opportunities during school breaks.

Organize a program with parent volunteers for teenagers, aged fourteen and fifteen, for excursions such as backpacking, orienteering, hiking, and swimming. Refer back to the survey you conducted earlier in the year to determine parental expertise. Many of your volunteers will be more than willing to lead these activities because of their vocations or hobbies.

14 Work with recreation services in the community.

Provide adult and youth summer programs, which could include gymnastics camp, movie matinees, crafts programs, and first aid instruction.

Allow for the open use of school computers and library facilities. Provide physical education facilities for use by fitness programs. Provide before- and afterschool activities at the school for students who would otherwise be left home alone.

15 Offer summer programs for preschoolers at the school.

Include activities such as games, crafts, storytelling, and educational video viewing. Meet two or three days a week for two hours a day. This provides for a stress-free introduction to the school building for parents and tots alike.

Work with your public library to see if they will participate in such a program.

16 Reinforce good behavior.

Have the adult supervisors (volunteers, educators, or support staff) carry a clipboard with them as they supervise the grounds. When students do something worth recognition or if they have a problem, have the supervisors record it. Celebrate positive student behaviors such as leadership, cooperation, responsibility, and helpfulness. Be sure that the positives as well as the negatives are dealt with in a proactive fashion.

17 Make schoolwide discipline an annual goal that is widely discussed.

All partners, including the students, should have their input considered. Follow well-researched training programs that outline appropriate behavioral expectations based on accepted principles such as logical consequences.

In addition, provide ongoing training to staff and parents to ensure the effectiveness of the plan once it has been implemented.

Recruiting Volunteers

Recruitment of volunteers should be an ongoing activity that is not done in isolation. Be proactive and realistic when determining the number of parents who will be involved.

Broaden requests for volunteer involvement to social service agencies, senior citizen homes, high schools, colleges, and businesses. Do not turn down a prospective helper. Allow for flexibility in scheduling of activities and events to accommodate the schedules of volunteers.

Many parents work full time but want to contribute in some way to their child's education. It is the responsibility of the educators in the school to create opportunities for that to happen.

Make sure parents and members of the community know that the school has an open-door policy. Such a policy needs to be supported by demonstrating that when parents come to the school to discuss issues or concerns, or simply to visit, they feel welcome and that their needs will be addressed as soon as possible.

IDEAS TO USE

18 Advertise year-round for volunteers.

Make requests for both general assistance and help with specific activities or events. More volunteers will be attracted if they know what their potential roles will be in the program or event. Clearly define and advertise the expectations for volunteers. Tasks should be clearly outlined and include a time component. Be prepared to offer alternative volunteer activities. Keep in mind that some parents may not be able to come to school to help but would be willing to undertake tasks they could do at home.

Start the conversation by asking parents if they could contribute even one hour a year. This starts the dialogue. It is important to follow through with any volunteers who agree to contribute.

19 Employ a structured approach to involving parents.

Use systems or structures. You could select volunteers by geographic location or draft every third parent alphabetically from a class list.

Create telephone fan-outs or an e-mail Listserv to ensure that everyone is informed of the opportunities to become a part of the school community.

To use a telephone fan-out, have the first parent call two parents and share the specified information. Then those two parents each call two more parents. Then the four parents each call two more, and so on. No parent has to call more than two other individuals, and the information is quickly shared. A plan outlining who calls who (as well as alternate phone numbers) should be designed at the beginning of the school year.

Ask committed volunteers to bring a friend who is interested in volunteering to an orientation session.

20 Use personal contact.

Personalize the invitation to parents about volunteer opportunities by using handwritten notes by students, other parents, teachers, or administrators. Make telephone calls if time permits. A telephone fan-out ensures that all parents are contacted and the responsibility does not fall on one or two individuals.

21 Advertise the need for volunteers.

Access community and business newsletters and Web sites. Ask the local chamber of commerce, grocery stores, real estate agencies, and doctors and dentists offices for space on their bulletin boards, newsletters, or Web sites.

This request will be accommodated more readily if you have established a positive relationship with local organizations.

22 Offer job sharing.

Time commitments may curtail parent involvement. Offer the opportunity for parents to share a volunteer assignment. A mother with a newborn at home may not be able to commit to a three-hour stretch as library parent, but may be able to give an hour and a half with the remainder of the shift staffed by another parent. Facilitate interaction between parents so that such arrangements may be made.

The initial organization of this job scheduling is critical because, done properly, it will ensure that volunteers can fulfill their responsibilities. At elementary schools, staff can work in conjunction with members of the parent advisory council; at middle and secondary schools, consider using student leaders in conjunction with parent organizers.

23 Consider employing a full-time trained volunteer coordinator for your district or school.

This idea may or may not be feasible, depending on budget. However, it may be possible to recruit a parent who is willing to make a substantial commitment of time serving as volunteer coordinator. Provide this volunteer with the appropriate training and resources, such as access to support staff, a computer, and office supplies.

24 Hold a volunteer fair.

Have booths that represent various volunteer programs. For instance, include a booth for the PTA and another for the Parent Boosters Club. Advertise the fair to the entire community. Hold it in conjunction with another school event that is likely to attract parents, students, and alumni (such as a football homecoming game).

Duplicate the opportunities by holding a virtual volunteer fair as well as the traditional type.

Meeting the Needs of Volunteers

I t is not enough to recruit parents and community members to assist at the school. It is necessary for educators to make a conscious effort to meet the needs of individuals who volunteer their time. Create a school climate where volunteers have a sense of belonging. Parents need to feel they are welcomed and supported.

The most effective way to meet the needs of volunteers is to ask, "What do you need, and how can we help support you in your role as a volunteer?" In addition, spend time getting to know the community. Successful volunteer programs are those that proactively try to eliminate barriers to parent participation wherever possible.

IDEAS TO USE

25 Meaningfully involve volunteers in planning projects.

It is important that the involvement meets the needs of not only the staff but also the volunteers. To ensure that two-way communication occurs, some basic procedures need to be established.

Train a few past volunteers to serve in leadership "liaison" roles to discuss what volunteering entails and how volunteers need to work with staff toward common goals.

Planning

Do a needs assessment with support teachers, administrators, and support staff. For example, teachers could answer the following kinds of questions to delineate what they need in terms of support.

Questions for classroom teachers:

- How do you want parents involved in the classroom? Outline the amount of time you need volunteers during the course of a week.
- List activities you want support for in the classroom. For example,
    working with small groups
    preparing instructional materials
    working with individual students
- What activities could be done at the volunteer's home?
- Do you need support for classwide activities such as field trips? In-class social activities? If so, how frequently?
- How will you communicate with the volunteers?

Keep the parent volunteers' level of involvement in a range that is comfortable for both volunteers and staff.

It is important to be aware of any collective agreements that impact the type of involvement that may take place.

26 Meaningfully involve volunteers in implementing projects.

Implementing

Use a core group of parents to develop the plan of where and when the volunteers work. After the roster is available, a schedule needs to be developed that aligns the staff needs with volunteer requests. For example, at the elementary school level many parents want to work in the classroom. At the middle school and secondary levels, students are often sensitive to parents working in the classroom (although they do enjoy the presence of their parents around the school, despite their protestations).

It must be emphasized that volunteering is a commitment, and if individuals cannot fulfill their commitment, the school needs to be informed. By the same token, staffs must be prepared when volunteers come to help by having materials and directions ready.

Make sure volunteers have a place to meet in the school and a method of obtaining refreshments. I have seen many schools establish "parent rooms" where parents can bring their children and work. This room has available resources, current professional reading materials, and accessible refreshments. It is often furnished with toys so parents can bring their preschool children with them while they volunteer.

27 Evaluate volunteer and staff performance and give appropriate feedback.

It is important to know both the volunteers and the staff well enough to tailor the evaluation with a focus on improvement.

A volunteer and staff self-evaluation can help define the role performed by the individual and communicate a volunteer's impressions of the school and the assignment. Staff evaluation will ensure that they are using volunteers effectively and possibly deal with potential problems.

All evaluations and feedback should be constructive and seek to promote growth and understanding.

28 Timing is everything.

Plan for joint evaluations before the winter break, before spring break, and at year's end. A simple way to evaluate would be to do a 1-2-3 approach that both the staff member and the volunteer fill out individually and then discuss together.

- List one challenge of the volunteer program.
- List two things that worked well in the program.
- List three things that would strengthen the program.

The key to this type of evaluation is the discussion that takes place after the staff and volunteers complete the evaluation. It will enhance the partnership by strengthening the relationship between the staff and volunteers.

Training Volunteers

Orient and train volunteers to ensure that they are comfortable in their roles, feel competent in their assigned responsibilities, and know that they are valued. In addition, present the volunteer program as an opportunity for individuals to gain skills and experience.

Create opportunities for volunteers to network with other volunteers, be involved in social activities, and be celebrated for their continued contribution. Providing volunteers with specific feedback about their performance will strengthen the role volunteerism plays in the school.

IDEAS TO USE

29 Host orientation sessions for volunteers.

Schedule two tours a year (one in September and one in January). Have seasoned volunteers conduct the school tours and be sure each volunteer is introduced to every staff member.

Build a virtual tour of the school for those who cannot be available for the scheduled times. Follow up with a chat session to answer any questions.

30 Develop a code of ethics for volunteers.

Use input from the teaching staff and from the volunteers to develop the code. Focus on confidentiality issues such as discussing individual students' progress and student records. Include expectations regarding health and safety issues. Outline school policies such as the prohibition of smoking and drinking on school grounds.

31 Publish a volunteer handbook.

If you do not have a handbook in place, the actual development of one by parents and staff should be the first step in the training process.

Clarify the role of volunteers. Enunciate expectations such as attendance and confidentiality. Provide relevant information such as volunteer sign-in procedures, conflict resolution strategies, and methods of evaluation. In addition, be sure volunteers receive the school safety procedures, student disciplinary code, volunteers' code of ethics, and a map of the building and grounds.

32 Provide instructional training for volunteers.

Include topics such as teaching styles, conflict resolution, instructional technology, and curriculum and instruction. In addition to acquiring training on how to contribute to school life, volunteers (and other family members) want to know and understand the curriculum of the school as it directly impacts the educational life of their children.

Because of the expertise of the educators, sharing knowledge with parents should be simply a matter of establishing the time and place of volunteer opportunities. My belief is that educators do have a professional responsibility to engage in the development of parents.

Here are some suggestions for middle school parent sessions.

Middle School Parent Sessions

• Student leadership opportunities with an eye to understanding the middle school culture (special events, intramurals, extracurricular). Share with parents how they can be involved.

- Advisory programs. Explain what they are and how they help students gain a sense of acceptance at the middle school.

- Bullying. Share strategies to deal with the behavior from both perspectives—that of being the bully and that of being bullied.

- Developmental needs of adolescents. Discuss the social, emotional, and cognitive levels of adolescents.

- Learning outcomes for information literacy. Parents could be informed of state/provincial standards, instructional delivery, and student assessment in the area of technology.

- Teaching strategies for gifted children. Discuss guidelines for identifying, understanding, and reaching gifted adolescents.

- Articulation from elementary to middle to high school. Share the plans that are in place to transition students. Discuss orientation, social events, time tables, and buddy systems. In other words, what are the similarities and what are the differences in the school organizations? This will help parents work with their children to understand the changes they face. Ongoing curriculum updates ensure that parents feel connected to their children's education.

Developing Staff

S taff members need to be trained on how to work with volunteers the same as volunteers need to understand the role and responsibilities they have committed to.

A good resource that provides insight into developing working relationships with parents is by Gwen Rudney (2005) in *Every Teacher's Guide to Working With Parents.* In discussing what parents want from teachers, she states:

> The top two answers—listed by approximately 90% of the parents—are linked to the learning environment and beyond. The two things parents want first and foremost are that the teachers care about their children and know them as individuals. The desire for these qualities reveals how sensitive parents are to their children's emotional needs and how deep their concern is about their children's lives at school. (p. 37)

Knowing why volunteers want to be involved with the school is fundamental to a successful relationship.

IDEAS TO USE

33 Provide staff with an inservice, focusing on working effectively with volunteers.

As a school-based administrator of a community school, I believed that all teachers would automatically want volunteers to be involved in the classroom. This, I learned, was not a correct assumption, and I discovered that, in fairness to teachers, they need the opportunity to learn about working with volunteers as much as volunteers need to have support in preparing them for their role.

Therefore, start the discussion about volunteerism by providing the opportunity for teachers to decide the degree of volunteer involvement that works most effectively for student learning in their classroom. Student learning always needs to be the priority.

The culture of each school should be based on the premise that parents and families are partners in the educational process and have a right as well as a responsibility to be involved. However, staff members need to be reassured that volunteers will not comment on their teaching styles, on personality issues, or on individual students. If a problem does occur, the staff should have a mechanism in place to bring about an amicable resolution.

Key issues that should be developed for teacher training sessions include the discussion about the different types of involvement for volunteers. Constructing this part of the training around the six types of volunteering reported in *School, Family, and Community Partnerships: Your Handbook for Action* by Joyce Epstein et al. (1997) would be a good framework to use with the staff (see Part 4).

Discussions in such sessions could focus on key components such as

- how to develop clear expectations for volunteers. For example, volunteers can prepare instructional materials, work with students, set up labs for instructional experiences such as science experiments, arrange drivers for field trips, or a combination of all of the above and more.
- what resources and directions to have prepared.
- how the scheduling of the volunteers should be done.

- what volunteerism looks like for each person.
- expectations around time commitment. For example, there could be periods of time that no volunteers should be in the class because of the type of instruction occurring (e.g., test taking).
- how the communication between volunteers will take place. To imply that every situation is going to be perfect is unrealistic. Who the staff talks to and what process is used if there are difficulties needs to be in place before volunteering starts.

Note that most parents are often nervous about working in the classroom, and teachers are often nervous about having them there. Dealing with that issue up front in a staff training session would help alleviate possible problems.

34 Be responsible and accountable.

As mentioned earlier, staff have responsibilities to their volunteers, which include the following:

- Preparing an appropriate amount of work
- Providing the directions and materials needed to do the assignment
- Offering some variety in the tasks
- Communicating expectations
- Maintaining a schedule
- Facilitating a full understanding of classroom routines, limits, and special needs
- Showing appreciation

35 Know volunteers as individuals.

It would be helpful if the volunteers and the staff had an opportunity for a two-way interview and were able to discuss the following:

- The type of skills and talents volunteers possess
- Methods to ensure that volunteers feel welcome in the school and in the classroom
- The concerns volunteers have about assuming a volunteer position and the concerns educators have about involving them
- The process to use in communicating with each other

Volunteers who feel they are appreciated and valued as individuals as well as for their contributions will be strong advocates for the school.

Placing and Supporting Volunteers

P arents do not always have the time or resources to be directly involved in their child's education. Therefore, the time parents are involved should be spent doing meaningful tasks. Schools that recognize parent barriers to involvement and make a concerted effort to reach parents benefit from increased involvement and support. Such efforts enhance the belief that the staff want parents to be involved. The British Columbia Confederation of Parent Advisory Councils *Advocacy Report* (BCCPAC, 1998) identified the several barriers parents have in dealing with the school system. Some of the key ones were poor communication, lack of time, lack of knowledge about district and school policies/procedures, and not knowing the rights of students and the responsibilities of staff.

Volunteers are just that, volunteers. They are spending their own time to assist the school in order to help children. Educators need to respect their commitment by consulting with them and adapting assignments to fit volunteers' schedules and time constraints. Keep in mind that the staff should know in advance what they want the volunteers to do and how it is to be accomplished.

Some parents become disenchanted with volunteering when they are given less than meaningful tasks. Therefore the placement of parents needs to be thought through to ensure that volunteers stay involved and committed. The worst public relations scenario for a school is to have volunteers become disgruntled and cease volunteering.

In addition, be clear about what the teaching and support staff union regulations say about the activities volunteers may perform.

IDEAS TO USE

36 Consider the following questions when placing volunteers.

- What kind of time commitment can the person make?
- How well does the individual relate to others?
- What skills or talents does the person possess?
- What are the possible frustrations or benefits of the different tasks assigned volunteers?
- What types of teaching styles exist in the placement situations?
- What has been the past experience of others with the volunteer?
- What are the preferences of the staff and the volunteers?

37 Provide free child care to encourage parents to come to school activities.

In order for parents to take full advantage of free child care, the arrangement for the care needs to be explicit and well communicated in advance.

Be clear about where the children should be taken, who will be looking after them, what entertainment will be provided, and what the hours of operation are. Provide a contact name and number so spots can be reserved.

The advisory council can coordinate this with staff at the elementary school, and in middle or secondary schools it can be coordinated with members of the student council.

38 Facilitate baby-sitting pools for parents who want to spend some time volunteering in the school.

Arrangements can be made for families to take turns baby-sitting each other's children so that they may spend time volunteering at the school. The key to this strategy is to have someone take responsibility for organizing the baby-sitting pool. It may be between parents in a class on a particular day, or for a certain period of time on a weekly basis. Be creative with the parameters. This is a good initiative for a parent advisory council to coordinate, as it creates a win-win situation for all involved.

39 Provide refreshments to volunteers to engender a feeling of comfort.

Although this may sound like a statement of the obvious, when volunteers know they may help themselves to a cup of coffee and a snack, it symbolizes a culture of comfort and belonging. It is important to acknowledge the work done by volunteers through such tokens of appreciation.

40 Offer transportation alternatives to parents without cars.

Facilitate car pools. When an invitation is made to come to school, it should, whenever possible, include transportation options (local bus routes and times as well as numbers to call for a ride). Check to see if the district bus service can run a special route for parents when activities are being held at school.

Acknowledging Volunteers

I t is important to positively reinforce parents by acknowledging their role in the school. Parents and other family members volunteer their time to improve the quality of school life. Systemic methods should be in place that make volunteers feel welcome and demonstrate that their opinions and contributions are valued. Recognition is important because, if volunteers do not feel appreciated, they will not stay involved. Acknowledgment does not require a major effort but will have a major payoff.

The demonstration of appreciation needs to be a clearly stated school or district objective to ensure that it is not overlooked. Seek volunteer input to determine relevant and meaningful displays of appreciation.

IDEAS TO USE

41 Catch individuals in the act of volunteering.

Use the school camera, a video camera, or yearbook photographer to take pictures of volunteers. Find appropriate ways to display the pictures. Create a photo collage, a slide show, or a DVD or video for the final appreciation event. Use bulletin boards and school Web sites to express appreciation and show who is involved. Remember: photos always make a nice marketing presentation for new recruits.

In the staff lounge, list the accumulated weekly or monthly total number of volunteer hours to date. This strategy is a visible representation of the level of volunteer commitment and publicly acknowledges volunteers' ongoing contribution. One way to document the hours is a sign-up sheet at the office as individuals come into the school and pick up their volunteer identification. This is also a helpful method of knowing who is in the school and helps ensure student safety.

Acknowledge and profile volunteers in the school newsletters and yearbook. Recognize a volunteer of the month or week.

42 Hold an annual recognition event.

The event could take the form of a luncheon, tea, or dinner. Consider an all-school assembly where volunteers are honored through skits and songs. Present volunteers with tokens of appreciation (if possible, ones made by students, such as place mats or cards).

Here is an example of an inexpensive yet personal token. As a staff you could hand out bags of mints with a card reading, "You are worth a mint." Add a personalized note about the contribution the individual made.

43 Replace visitors' buttons or tags with "VIP" buttons.

The Very Important Person message will certainly convey that volunteer contributions are important. Make sure the buttons are picked up in a central location where the volunteers sign in and log their hours.

44 Send personalized thank-you and/or birthday notes.

Make sure a system is in place to do this, whether it is the responsibility of the volunteer coordinators, students, administration, or teachers.

I always like to send at least one note of appreciation through regular mail, as it is always refreshing to receive an unexpected thank-you card.

Volunteers will appreciate the fact that you have taken the time to personalize the note.

45 Feature parent volunteers and their contributions, as well as volunteer programs, on the school and district Web sites.

The school Web site should be used as a basic communication tool for volunteers. Design a "volunteer link," where individuals can find information about specific volunteer programs. Incorporate information about the contacts in charge of the volunteers (depending on how you have organized them—by grade level, classroom, program, subject, office support, and administrative help). Provide the name and contact information.

Include upcoming events and what the volunteer needs are related to each activity. Be sure to be specific about who to contact, how to volunteer, as well as the specific ways volunteers will be needed. Such detail allows individuals to make informed decisions.

It is important to align district and school volunteer activities. Many of the districts you work in have district parent advisory councils. Work in concert with them to advertise and acknowledge the special volunteers and the programs that you have at your school.

46 Put a different class/different grade level in charge of honoring volunteer efforts each month.

Part of creating a culture that values family involvement is to have the students recognize and acknowledge the role volunteers play in their education. Although many students in middle school and secondary schools state they do not want their parents in school, research shows parent involvement increases student achievement at these levels. The following was stated in a National PTA (2005) article titled "Don't Talk to Me, My Friends Are Watching":

> The reasons for this decline in parent involvement just as teens are entering middle and high schools is two-fold. First, maturing children have a growing need to develop a sense of self and independence that is separate from their families. They begin to weigh choices and consequences, make more decisions on their own, learn from their mistakes, and establish their own set of values to guide their decisions and actions. They begin refusing help from their parents and don't want them along when they're with friends.
>
> Second, parents' roles begin changing, too, in order to allow for their children's self-identity development. While parents continue to offer support and love, they begin stepping back a little in all aspects of their children's lives in order to show their respect for their children's growing independence. Parents must begin to let adolescents make their actions and decisions. (paras. 2, 3)

As a result, there is often a drop in the involvement of parents after elementary school. It then becomes even more of a challenge for schools to find ways to involve parents.

By involving students in organizing and honoring the involvement of volunteers, there will be more acceptance and understanding of the contributions made by their families.

Activities could range from preparing acknowledgments on the school Web site to strawberry teas, thank-you notes, and plays and skits in school assemblies. Challenge the creativity of the grade levels/classes to find ways to acknowledge and appreciate contributions.

PART 2

Creating the Climate

Charles Teddlie and David Reynolds (2000) provide a profile of characteristics that identify a school as effective or ineffective. An effective school has strong leadership, focused teaching and learning, high expectations for all, an emphasis on students' rights and responsibilities, a site-specific plan for developing staff, and strong parent involvement. To ensure that parent involvement is in place, there must be a climate for such involvement.

Creating that accepting climate requires trust among students, teachers, support staff, parents, and administrators. This requires a concerted effort made at all levels of the organization, as parents can be very skeptical about the quality of education offered to their children. The key to success is trust and respect of one another's roles in the education of children.

Jane Huffman and Kristine Hipp (2003) identify trust as a key factor in building a learning community. It is critical that educators take the leadership role in communicating and involving parents, and not just in a superficial way. Know your community. It is important that you understand the culture of the community you work in. As one of my colleagues commented when discussing how to involve families, "Call early and call often." A system that is truly collaborative has a variety of infrastructures in place, from the boardroom to the classroom, that facilitates such an enterprise.

Projecting a Positive Image

Develop a specific plan that will show the school in a positive light and highlight the strengths of the programs. Be clear about the school's and the district's goals when planning such strategies. Make certain that any plan highlights the school's role in the academic, social, emotional, aesthetic, and physical development of students and the community.

There is no question that educators must constantly communicate that wonderful teaching and learning take place every day in schools. Elaine McEwan (2003) in her research determined ten traits of highly effective administrators. The first trait she discusses is that of being a communicator, "a genuine and open human being with the capacity to listen, empathize, and connect with individual students, parents and teachers in productive, helping and healing ways" (p. xxx).

The recognition of the different beliefs, cultures, and values of the families attending the school should affect the design of the message.

Remember that nothing makes a school look better than polite, well-mannered, and contributing students.

IDEAS TO USE

47 Create a physical atmosphere in the school and grounds that is friendly and inviting.

Offer reading material and comfortable chairs in reception areas, extensively display student work, and hang "welcome" signs in languages that are appropriate for the community. Install a marquee to advertise upcoming events and recognize student and teacher accomplishments for the whole neighborhood to see.

48 Do an informal audit.

Invite two or three community members (alumni and/or business leaders) who do not have children in the school system to visit the school. Ask the auditors the following questions after they tour the facility:

- What was your initial impression of the school?
- Did you feel comfortable coming to the school?
- Were there friendly faces, helpful staff, and polite students?
- How do the facilities and grounds rate in terms of cleanliness, signage, and availability of parking?
- What other observations do you have?

Have them meet with a representative partner group (teachers, parents, students, and administrators) to discuss their findings. Ask them if they have suggestions for improvement. Discuss with the auditors what procedure will be used to further share and act on their findings.

49 Offer articulation meetings for parents of matriculating students.

Articulation meetings are designed to ease the transition for students moving from one school to another (elementary to middle school or middle school to secondary school). Typically, school administrators along with relevant staff host a parent meeting where expectations of parents and staff may be "articulated." It is important to include tours of the middle and secondary schools as part of the articulation process.

Although this will be a standard process for most schools, the manner in which the meetings are conducted will create a first impression that will last with prospective parents and students. Welcoming faces and an open invitation to be a part of the school will start a student's and parent's journey on a very positive note.

Use PowerPoint or a DVD presentation to orient new students and parents. Highlight school events, projects, and activities and emphasize the uniqueness of the school. Include school rules and procedures. Providing the new student with links to the teacher's class could also be a part of the presentation. The teacher could explain any rules, procedures, or any other important information that the new students and parents need to know.

Make sure that parents and families understand how welcome and needed they are in the life of the school.

50 Welcome midyear transfers.

Devise your own brand of "welcome wagon." Provide new students and their parents with information on the surrounding community as well as on the school. The materials can be sent through the mail or posted on the school Web site, or you could schedule a courtesy call to a new arrival's home. Representatives of the advisory council, school counselors, or an administrator should conduct the home visit.

51 Offer adult programs during the school day.

Work with the district's continuing education department or the representatives of the local community college to determine appropriate course offerings. They could range from cooking, fitness, and fashion design classes to skill-enhancement and job preparedness classes.

Be proactive before offering the program and be aware that parents may perceive student safety issues. Deal with safety issues in an up-front and forthright manner.

52 Involve students in community projects.

Have students provide services to senior citizens (cutting lawns, shopping for groceries, running errands); volunteer in public institutions such as libraries, hospitals, and hospices; or support community initiatives such as reclaiming park lands and restocking lakes.

Friendly competitions at middle schools between teams to collect hours of community service can be beneficial to developing student citizenship as well as contributing to the life of the community.

Form partnerships with the Rotary Club, chamber of commerce, local hospitals, and nursing homes. Know your community and where services would be appreciated.

53 Prepare an enrollment information package.

In addition to general school information, include age-appropriate games, staff biographies, recipes for items such as homemade play dough, and school trivia questions that point out the unique character of the school.

54 Create a DVD or video starring the school.

Encourage middle or secondary school students through their electives to create a DVD/video or consider having professionals produce it. Many colleges and universities have students in film courses who would be delighted to be part of such a project.

Make multiple copies of the final product and disseminate to appropriate parties such as business partners, the chamber of commerce, and local realtors.

Show the DVD/video at parent-teacher conferences, articulation evenings, and other community events hosted by the school. Show it at malls, car dealerships, or any other accessible public venue.

55 Leave a legacy.

In English or language arts classes, ask students that are graduating (or leaving the top grade) to write letters of welcome to the new students coming to the school. Establish a structure for the letter writing by asking them to respond to questions such as the following.

- What should students remember to do on a daily basis?
- What is the best memory you have about the school?
- What is the one thing you wish you had known when you came to the school that you know now?
- What cautions do you have for students to ensure that they will be successful?

These letters could be used as part of the articulation process established by the school.

Marketing the Message

Marketing should be an expressed part of the school and district's action plans. The problem educators face is that the public is not as informed as they should be about the quality of the job the public education system is doing. Consider the fact that, in many instances, public support is needed to approve bond issues to fund schools. Unfortunately, the majority of the public cannot see the need for additional funding because they are unaware of what is taking place within schools. Educators need to take responsibility for communicating with the public and be more proactive in doing so; they should continually inform the public about both what is going well and what challenges the school is facing.

Use the following strategies to demonstrate to parents that educators are more than willing to discuss education with them and that the school doesn't have all the answers but educators are willing to learn and problem solve with parents. Allyson Van Fleet (2005) states that in order for the message to be received by all intended audiences, a mixture of communication methods must be used and matched to your audience.

IDEAS TO USE

56 Establish contact with the local media.

Invite members of the media to all school events. Don't forget to provide invitations to both sporting events and events with an academic focus, such as science fairs and college bowl competitions. Include media representatives in volunteer appreciation efforts during the course of the year or plan a separate media-relations lunch.

If at all possible, form a partnership with the local media and publish a weekly or biweekly newsletter, "Breaking News at Elementary, Middle, or Secondary X School." Contributors should come from a variety of sources such as individual students or staff, classes, the parent advisory council, and student councils.

The key to the success of such a newsletter is to have someone be responsible for coordinating the articles and submitting them on a regular basis.

57 Use volunteers to help distribute information.

Remember, a majority of the residents of the community do not have children in school. Share the school's successes, goals, and plans. Develop a plan to have volunteers go door to door several times a year to deliver programs, bulletins, and newsletters.

Advertise the school Web site. Share the e-mail address of the key communicators in your school. Be prepared to respond to questions and concerns of all taxpayers.

58 Assemble an ongoing photomontage.

This could take the form of a memory book or a classroom or hall display. Include a variety of shots from academic endeavors to community service. Ask parents throughout the year to send their digital pictures that they take at school events. Display the photos in a place where the whole school and its visitors may enjoy them.

Put the photomontage in a PowerPoint DVD presentation and distribute to parents via the school Web site for downloading and/or e-mail it as an attachment.

59 Read the handwriting on the wall.

Place large graffiti sheets (chart paper or newsprint) on the walls in an area where all volunteers have access (such as the office reception area, hallway, or foyer). Have marking pens available for ad hoc comments. Consider focusing the input each week by having specific headings on the graffiti sheets.

Ask for strengths as well as areas of growth.

60 Foster discussion about education with parents.

Survey parents on the following topics. You can ask some or all of these questions over the course of the school year.

- What concerns do you have about your child's education?
- What are the strengths of the education system in relation to your child's education?
- What do you expect from classroom teachers? School administrators? Counselors? Support staff?
- How do you keep your child accountable for his or her learning?
- What is your role in your child's schooling?
- How does your child learn best?

Remember to respond to parent comments.

61 Publish and circulate a classroom newsletter.

Include suggestions for helping with homework and a "Coming Up" section to get parents and students ready for the next chapter or topic. Share curriculum updates and use this as a vehicle to establish two-way communication.

Make the newsletter specific to what is taking place in your classroom.

62 Create a class home page as a link on the school or district Web site.

Include the same kind of information that would be included in a class newsletter as above, but update more frequently.

Give daily homework tips. Suggest other Web sites to explore. Not only is this a good way to use all that technology has to offer, but it can also serve as an entrée for a discussion of Internet safety for young people.

Set up office hours for parents to chat with you on a weekly or biweekly basis or use Blackboard to set up a discussion board.

63 Spruce up parent meetings.

Try different formats at your meetings by using effective teaching strategies. Present ideas and information or trigger discussion through displays, charts, DVD presentations or videos, collages, murals, cartoons, artifacts, photographs, games, skits, or scrapbooks.

Use cooperative learning strategies such as Think, Pair, Share or 2-4-8.

For example, you may want parents to discuss how to plan an outdoor camping trip for students, and to do this, you need to develop some common expectations for student behavior. This particular 2-4-8 strategy involves having two people share, and then decide what rules they agree on. Then four people share, and the four have to come to an agreement. You can use this strategy with up to eight people. Take the behaviors each group of eight have agreed on, and most likely you will achieve your goal of establishing expectations very quickly (as well as having parents engage in some very good conversation around their expectations for their children).

64 Plan seminars for real estate agencies to introduce them to the schools in the district.

Many realtors will use the information they have about the school to sell homes. It is in your best interest to share all the positive results about the school.

Using Technology to Communicate

According to Frances Cairncross (2001), the Internet creates a new marketplace and a new information system as well as a new means of distribution and communication. There are technology systems that can be accessed by district staff, students, parents, and community with links to outside Web sites and resources. School and teacher Web sites can easily provide updates. This permits viewers to keep informed about what is happening in the school and in the classrooms.

Some parents will not have a computer. For those families, schools (and businesses) should consider donating second-generation computers. Many families would welcome these computers, as they will provide a basic method of getting online and accessing information. Collecting these computers could be a volunteer project.

Another way to have parents have equal access to computers is to have a parent meeting at the library so the librarian can show them how to use the computers there for free. Be sure to have transportation and child care for the parents who need it, and make a concerted effort to have families attend. Included are some sample ways to tap into the powerful world of technology.

IDEAS TO USE

65 Tap into district technologies.

Use e-mail to communicate with volunteers. This would include e-mailing requests for volunteers for general and specific needs, e-mailing newsletters and updates, and e-mailing information for quick communication.

Create a Web site that links to the district's main Web site. Assign pin numbers to parents so they can access their students' grades, homework assignments, newsletters, and any other pertinent information about their child, their classroom, and activities.

66 Create your own stars.

Share the information from the school's Web site on the television screen in the main entrance of the school so all visitors may view it as they enter. This could include advertisements about upcoming events. Imagine being able to see the winning championship basketball team as you stroll through the corridors of the secondary schools.

67 Global connections.

Virtual reality is here. Compressed video produces another range of opportunities for educators and their students. Internet-based face-to-face conversations can be created with people around the world, with the addition of a monitor-top or classroom video camera and video compression software. Students can watch a spacecraft travel to Mars or travel the Amazon River with a group of explorers. It is important that parents be a part of this journey.

Programs such as the Electronic Textbook allow educators and students to stay current with the latest technology. With the Internet, data are added every minute, and it is important that individuals have access up-to-date information and equipment.

68 Explore all the options.

There are unlimited kinds of computer software programs for remediation and enrichment in the classroom. School-based programs, parental involvement events, staff development, and grade-level meetings can all capitalize on Smart Boards, laptops, LCDs, and digital cameras. Leaders that are committed to technology use can be instrumental in enhancing the quality of education.

Teachers can post assignments and homework for students via a Web site. If students are absent due to sickness or some emergency, they may check the Web site for missed assignments. Also, the Web site could provide additional resource links for students to use.

69 Host virtual meetings.

There are many formats for setting up and managing e-mail discussion boards, such as Blackboard or Outlook Express. Virtual meetings will allow volunteers to participate in meetings without having to physically attend a meeting. This can encourage more parent involvement because they can respond at their leisure, whether at the office or late at night. While this type of setup is different from a face-to-face meeting, it is another way to provide an opportunity for input.

70 Make sure nothing is secret.

There are software systems that have a parent module that allows families with children in different schools to access all of the children's reports, homework, discipline, teacher comments, class and school announcements, and even what is on the menu in the cafeteria on a daily basis. The technology is available, but the challenge is for educators to be ready and willing to share that much information.

Communicating Effectively

Communication needs to be a two-way street. Ask parents what form of communication works best for them. Demonstrate the school's willingness to try different forms of communication to ensure that parent and student voices are being heard. When the lines of communication are open, students receive the message that the teachers and parents are partners in their education

According to Terry Pearce (2003),

> There's a huge difference between the opportunity to "have your say" and the opportunity to be heard. The good-to-great leaders understood this distinction, creating a culture wherein people had a tremendous opportunity to be heard and, ultimately, for the truth to be heard. (p. 43)

Be sure you understand that you not only must take into account that parents have a variety of reading levels but also have a knowledge of the primary languages used in the homes of your students.

According to Van Fleet (2005), the message must be sent out at least eight times to ensure it is communicated clearly and completely, and a variety of approaches should be used.

IDEAS TO USE

71 Be empathetic and keep an open mind.

Try to understand the position of the other person, whether it is a parent or a student. Pearce (2003) states that trust is a prerequisite for people to listen to others without fear or suspicion. Try not to solve the problem before all sides of the issue have been heard.

72 Provide opportunities for input.

Have a suggestion box posted in the school and encourage feedback from the parents, staff, students, and community. Use a telephone tree that operates on a systematic basis to seek as well as share information. Have a mechanism in place by which parents may contribute to the school's newsletter or Web site.

73 Keep the lines of communication open.

Consider the method used to communicate with parents when there is a student issue. Teachers should evaluate their level of effective communication by asking themselves these questions:

- When did I last talk to the student's parent?
- Was it a positive or negative message?
- How do I convey that it is the issue and not the student that I want to discuss?

74 Contact all parents by October.

Ask parents what method they prefer to establish and maintain ongoing communication. Use e-mail, cellular telephones, and pagers when possible.

Many times a parent is under the impression that the only time the school is in touch with them is when their child is in trouble. Change that perception through positive and reassuring phone calls.

75 Mail letters home occasionally.

A letter sent home in late August could be used as a means to welcome students who are brand new to the school or simply welcome all students to their new grade.

You could also use this method of communicating to outline the student's progress; include praise and areas of growth.

76 Invite parents and family members to assemblies.

Host a monthly or bimonthly assembly to celebrate positive student behavior and achievements.

Hand out certificates or an appropriate item such as a bookmark to acknowledge and reinforce positive student behavior.

Creating the Context for Change

Schools not only must change and grow themselves but also should encourage change and growth in the community they serve. Most persons do not like change and are thus unable to consider alternatives to a current method of operation. It is important to create a context for change and establish some common understandings among and between schools and parents.

The strategy that educators must take with families is demonstrating that the schools are authentic in their desire to involve and share the responsibility for providing quality education to their children, the students in the school. Terry Pearce (2003), in his book *Leading Out Loud: Inspiring Change Through Authentic Communication,* states:

> Authentic communication is a continual dance between the heart and the mind, and between you and those with whom you communicate. Your own engagement in the subject will provide a mirror of what you are engendering in others. As you are passionate, convinced, and committed about the change you want to make, so others can become passionate, convinced, and committed as they engage with you around your message. (p. 35)

According to Pearce (2003) you need to work with the parent community to establish the specific problems that need to be addressed. After identifying the issues, come to consensus about what action is needed and what information the group needs to know to solve the problem.

IDEAS TO USE

77 Pick a number.

In groups of six to eight, brainstorm five words or ideas under the following headings: Language, Values, Technology, and Parenting. Give the group ten to fifteen minutes to list items that underscore what is different today as compared with twenty years ago. The facilitator selects one word under each column. For example, use word 2 under Language, use word 4 under Values, use word 5 under Technology, and word 3 under Parenting.

Have the group use these words to write a statement about change. Allow them to be funny or serious. Hand out long strips of paper and have each group write the statement out, sign their names to it, and post it on the wall. As the participants break for refreshments, they can circulate and read the other groups' statements.

This exercise is a powerful way to introduce a discussion about change and the impact it has on education. I have used it a number of times to generate dialogue around educational expectations, from the view of both the parents and the educators.

78 Connect the variables.

Each parent is asked to reflect upon the relationship between student achievement and the following: teachers' expectations, parents' expectations, economic status, parental involvement, and attendance. Have them discuss their comments in groups of four. Then have the groups formulate a statement about student achievement.

Parents often need a chance to voice their concerns and hear other points of view before they are willing to discuss possible solutions. Remember that a person's perception is their truth.

79 Throw them a lifeline.

Often, comparing the way things were to the way they are now, and seeing what the commonalities are, helps parents discuss and clarify issues they may have regarding change. Use activities to create a context, or mindset, for educational change. In addition, these ideas offer a way to lead from a general discussion on change to a specific issue that needs to be addressed.

Have participants in groups of six (or fewer) draw a horizontal line on a blank sheet of paper. Have them use it as their lifeline from birth to their current age. Ask them to individually draw vertical lines at appropriate places on the line to mark key events in their lives. After that is done, have them identify two or three life events that most affected their attitudes toward education. For example, many will discuss having children, or dropping out of school, or a particular teacher that taught them. Discuss the impact this event had and what changed for them as a result.

Relate the personal changes in life to the changes faced in education. Use this idea at a meeting where some change in education that may be controversial and require parental support will be discussed.

80 Employ a Venn diagram to initiate a discussion about change.

Label two overlapping circles "Schools Twenty Years Ago" and "Schools Today" respectively. First, ask participants to work in groups of three to define the nonintersecting areas. In the left area, they outline what schools were like twenty years ago, and in the right area, they outline what schools are like

Venn Diagram

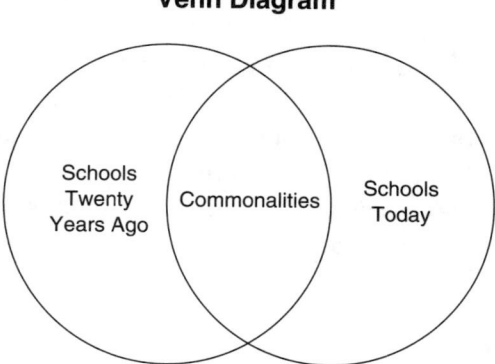

today. In the area of intersection, they list the commonalities between the two eras. Allow fifteen to twenty minutes for the completion of the diagrams, and then ask the groups to share their work. List the various groups' responses.

81 Ensure random seating.

On some occasions it is important that parents mix and do not just sit with the same group of persons they know. Random seating stimulates a cross-fertilization of ideas and opens discussion.

Often when parents come to a meeting they come with someone they know and do not like to be separated from them. Know that the previously mentioned activities take people out of their comfort zones and make it "risky" for some. Therefore it is important to link these activities to the main content of the session, or participants will perceive these activities as a waste of time.

82 Get it together.

Enlarge five cartoons to 8½-by-11-inch size using a photocopier with enlargement capability. Cut each cartoon into six pieces. The number of cartoons will depend on the number of groups to be created. As parents arrive, hand them a piece of a cartoon. They have to find the five other persons that have the pieces of the same cartoon and form a group. On each table, have a glue stick and a felt pen. Have the group glue the cartoon on a sheet of paper and write a caption under it relating to the topic of the meeting.

Once they have finished, have each group post their cartoon at the front of the room and then sit together in their group.

83 Spill the beans.

Have different colored jelly beans (groups of six of the same color) in a dish. Have each person take a jelly bean as they come in the door. A person sits in a group at the table that has a dish of jelly beans matching the color he or she has selected. As parents join the group, have each person introduce himself or herself to the other members.

PART 3

Sustaining the Involvement

R od Paige (2002) observed that parents are children's first and most important teachers, and it is important that all parents build and keep strong ties to their children's schools. When parents and families are involved in their children's schools, the children behave better and have better attitudes about going to school.

Difficulties related to parental involvement (such as declining numbers of parent volunteers, frustration with roles, unresolved conflicts, and dissatisfaction with the school) occur when educators do not treat families as partners. Because some teachers and administrators do not want parents to interfere in what they see as the professional's domain, parents are often kept at arm's length.

Rick DuFour (2000), in his article "Community: Data Put a Face on Shared Vision," aligned the results of school achievement with the shared efforts of educators and all community members. He states that a school vision statement must address both the reality of a school and the sense of what the school could become. Therefore it is critical to incorporate respect for all cultures and all models of families. This should be evident in every aspect of the life of the school community. Educators need to be role models in this area.

Celebrating Diversity

I n *The Seven Habits of Highly Effective People*, Stephen Covey (1989) teaches a concept I have never forgotten. He explains that, rather than just accept and tolerate diversity, we need to celebrate it. The reality is that we live in a multicultural, multilingual world, and how educators handle this diversity is critical to the quality of education children receive. Values and beliefs are the decision-making filter that people use on a daily basis.

One of the reform efforts Beverly McLeod (1996) discusses is related to student diversity. She states,

> Now, as the U.S. economy has shifted from an industrial base to one requiring workers to possess technological and analytical skills, schools are being asked to prepare all students to read and write at a sophisticated level, to think critically and apply their knowledge to solving real-world problems, to work collaboratively with others, and to become lifelong learners. . . . Today, it is neither socially nor economically acceptable to be content with a minimal level of education for any group of students. The challenge is to provide equal educational opportunity to all students, regardless of differences among students in English proficiency and other characteristics.

Richardo Stanton-Salazar and Guadalupe Valdés (as cited in Romo, 2002) stated that different cultures have different expectations related to behavior, success, and the involvement of parents in their children's educational lives. This places a responsibility on the educators to not only know but also implement diverse ways of teaching and learning to support the values and beliefs of the cultures represented in their classrooms.

IDEAS TO USE

84 Provide staff development related to cultural differences.

In a culturally diverse school or district, focus staff development on ways to help educators succeed in involving families. This knowledge will support educators by making them aware of the significance of the decisions they make about student learning. Sara Lawrence-Lightfoot (2003), in an interview about her book *The Essential Conversation: What Parents and Teachers Can Learn From Each Other,* discussed the need to have educators develop their cultural awareness. She stated:

> All of the teachers that I spoke to said that they had received no preparation in their colleges or universities for working with the families of their students. Instead, they feel that they must make it up as they go along, without much guidance, mentoring, or support. . . . I can envision, for example, a wonderful course that might be called Teachers as Ethnographers in which the skills of listening, observing, and documenting are taught. . . . Teachers also need to learn to see and appreciate the parents' perspective, to step into their shoes. (para. 7)

85 Staff accordingly.

Staffing that includes bilingual members (teachers, administrators, and support staff) will create opportunities to provide multicultural role models. Staff can translate materials, do home visits, refer families to services, and generally support and provide assistance as needed.

86 Work with the whole family.

Create opportunities for parents to work with translators to ensure that all parents have input. The parent resource room is an ideal place for parents to network with each other as they support the school's volunteer projects.

The parents can also access the ESL classes established by either the school or community agencies.

87 Honor diversity in the curriculum.

In her study of school reform, Beverly McLeod (1996) discussed a school that established a monthly cross-cultural focus, in both core and elective subjects. She discussed the need for students to communicate in their own language. Where possible, it is important to offer classes in the students' native languages.

Acknowledge and respond to cultural celebrations such as Chinese New Year, Cinco de Mayo (a Mexican victory celebration that dates back to 1862), or Kwanzaa (a "first fruit" festival deriving from African practices).

Integrate the celebrations as part of your multicultural studies curriculum. Any of these events can be celebrated through poetry, dance, food, works of art, or the study of the history and rituals of the festivals.

Have students prepare for the event by selecting a culture they wish to study. Use print, audio, and video material and the Internet to gain information. This honors and celebrates diversity in your school community.

88 Help families access resources.

Interagency support has long been a part of the community school philosophy. Acting as a community center and outreach for families will enhance the quality of family life for those that need support. Facilitate contact with social services, mental health services, government agencies, and parenting workshops.

89 Design a variety of mediums.

Joanne Wojciuk (2005) discusses that because the workforce is both multilingual and multicultural employers are redesigning their benefits and service communications to reach the diverse population. She states that employers are realizing that translating brochures and Web site material into various languages is not enough. Cultural barriers must be considered when developing communication strategies. The school system faces this same challenge. Educators must consider how messages are received in the community, and the message must be delivered in a variety of mediums—and it may take research to determine the most effective methods.

90 Communicate clearly.

If there are language barriers and cultural barriers, it is critical that the purpose of the communication is shared in a clear and concise fashion at the beginning of the agenda. For example, clarify the purpose at the beginning of a meeting. In translated documents, state the purpose of the communication at the beginning. This simple concept is often overlooked in communication venues where educational lingo is involved. As educators, we have a language that can be confusing to people outside the profession. Educational leaders, sensitive to the issue of diversity, know the importance of communicating clearly and concisely.

91 Encourage families to host students from international exchange programs.

Many districts have international students that are part of the school system. The support provided by the sponsoring families of these students teaches an understanding and celebration of other cultures and also helps native students learn more about their own country because they serve as guides and hosts to their guests.

92 Sponsor a citizenship court or swearing-in ceremony for new citizens.

I have been a part of this ceremony in a high school auditorium. The event was hosted by a secondary school social studies class. It was an impressive opportunity to not only hear attributes of citizenship by guest speakers but also see the emotional reaction of new citizens. This is a rich experience that benefits students, teachers, and new citizens.

93 Support newcomers.

Many communities have organizations that help new immigrants adjust to their adoptive country. Make contact with organizations, such as the Travelers Aid Society or a local faith-based organization, and determine ways to work with and support the organizations in their efforts.

94 Define success.

Work with the parents and the community to find ways to celebrate the diversity of the community and understand the criteria of successful education. Harriet Romo (2002) writes:

We must encourage individuals who are meeting someone different from themselves or learning about an unfamiliar place to suspend judgment while getting to know the individual or place. We can assist students in understanding the role of evidence in the formation and justification of a viewpoint and help them weigh and evaluate evidence. We can encourage them to take stands on controversial issues based on evidence instead of commonly held stereotypes. (para. 19)

Using Community Resources

There are unlimited resources in a school community and a wide range of expertise that can be used to promote learning. It follows then that, by combining the wide range of skills, talents, and resources the community can offer with those of parents and teachers, the learning process is enhanced and enriched.

Integrate the use of community resources to support learning outcomes. Many businesses are more than willing to help and simply need to be approached, and involving seniors acknowledges their valuable contributions as citizens. Working with the larger community reinforces the principle that everyone is involved in education. Certainly, in this day and age, it is clearer than ever that "it takes a village to raise a child."

IDEAS TO USE

95 Ask parents and other interested members of the community to coach.

Recently I did some consulting work in a district and discovered a group of parents who had approached the secondary school in their community to form a parent coaching group. They worked with the school staff, administrators, and representatives of the district and unions to establish this group. Parents coach basketball, volleyball, mountain climbing, and other sports without teacher involvement. There was no challenge to the educator's role, but rather a respect for the fact that teachers could not do everything. This successful program has been in place for a number of years.

96 Model good citizenship.

Have student leaders approach the owners or managers of grocery stores and see if they will agree to the following proposal. For every $1,000 worth of receipts from that establishment that the students collect during a specified period of time, the store contributes $10 to a community food bank. Many parents would be more than willing to work with students to coordinate the project.

97 Host events that are sponsored by the community.

Two Examples

Hold a silent auction. Ask parents and the business community to contribute items for the auction. Be clear about how the funds raised will be used. Often, if such auctions are theme based, contributors and patrons will be pleased to participate.

Organize a pizza night. Partner with a local pizza place and designate a particular night as pizza night. Provide the business with advertising for the event and have the business respond by returning 15 to 20 percent of the sales as a donation to the school.

98 Include the senior members of the community.

It is important to involve all members of the family. "Adopt" seniors so that the school can share its resources and seniors can share theirs. Have seniors discuss their life stories from a historical perspective. Students could interview, write journals, or create videos of the experiences shared with the seniors. In return, students could teach interested seniors how to use computers.

Ask seniors to tutor students either at school or at senior centers. Offer a student reading service for seniors in return.

99 Offer free admission for senior citizens to school events such as sporting events and school plays.

Honoring seniors (the best community resource available) is something I think educators need to do. Seniors are such a valuable resource, and any way they can become part of the school culture will enrich the quality of students' education. I have watched seniors enjoy these events and become strong advocates for their local schools. If possible, organize transportation for them.

100 Organize safety patrols on Halloween night.

Volunteers could patrol either in well-marked vehicles or on foot from five o'clock to nine o'clock. This will help prevent school and community vandalism as well as protect the younger children from potential harassment. Coordinate efforts with the local police force. Give the volunteers treats to hand out as they patrol the streets.

101 Create a resource directory.

Start with the local telephone book and list those community resources (businesses, services, and governmental organizations) that could be used during the course of the year as a source of volunteers, sponsors, or sites to visit. Survey the staff members to see which resources they have used in the past and include the best sources in the directory. Keep track of how often a particular resource is used to prevent overtaxing that source's generosity.

Developing Community Relationships

Partnerships with community agencies, institutions, and organizations will give the school an increased sense of community identity. The more opportunities provided for parents and community members to be in the school, and the more opportunities for students to be in the community, the better.

Support the use of the school as the center for the community as a whole. Create opportunities for the community to communicate how they can support the school and how the school can support them. The mutual support and respect will pay a long-term dividend to both the school and business community.

IDEAS TO USE

102 Establish an art gallery in the school in cooperation with your local art club or association.

Students can showcase their masterpieces in the school hallways along with those of local artists. This project creates the benefits of profiling the fine arts in school as well as being aesthetically pleasing. Local artists may even be inspired to donate pictures to the school for permanent display. I saw this idea work effectively at a middle school, and parents, teachers, and students stood in awe at the students' artistic talents as they viewed their art amidst the array of fine work of local artists.

This activity works particularly well in middle and secondary schools, as there are specific art programs that can coordinate the program. Set a time limit for art displays. This will inspire a constant flow of viewers to see what is newly displayed.

103 Use the school as a student employment center.

Offer student services such as painting, gardening, babysitting, and pet sitting. Use the school newsletter, Web site, and the local media to advertise the services. Have students prepare a résumé as part of the program.

This can be coordinated by career preparation or work experience programs at the secondary schools.

At the elementary and middle schools, work with the student council and the parent council to coordinate the service. Student safety must be ensured when this type of program is established.

104 Involve the school in program registration for nonprofit organizations.

Guides, scouts, and the local parks and recreation department may want to take advantage of the school's hospitality. These nonprofit organizations that serve the community are often pressed for meeting space.

105 Hold a summer reading exchange.

Invite parents and students to swap both children's and adult books prior to the summer recess. Include materials from the school library that have been weeded from its collection.

106 Support the season.

Community service agencies need the support of schools to help fill their mandates, especially during the holiday season.

Canvass businesses to determine what services they would provide to families in need (e.g., haircuts, dry-cleaning, and car repairs). Have students collect nonperishable foods and either prepare hampers or donate the foods to local charities for distribution.

107 Establish community information centers.

In these centers, provide current information on local organizations and government, social services agencies, community events, and any other community resources.

Include information on adult education, health services, social services, and law enforcement. Link these evenings with other more traditional evenings such as Meet the Teacher night. It will not only help attendance but also demonstrate the positive relationship the school has with the community at large.

Host community services information evenings to inform your school community of available resources.

108 Always be prepared.

There is a very valuable and essential role for parents to play in developing an emergency preparedness plan for home and school. Invite parents to hear guest speakers or to raise money to purchase emergency kits or a truck container to house earthquake and emergency supplies.

109 Sponsor community forums.

Community forums could include election debates (district, municipal, state, or federal candidates); municipal issues such as bond issues, parks, roads, and budget; and school district issues such as literacy, truancy, or student retention.

Be sure that if the school hosts election forums, all sides are invited to participate.

Students may act as hosts, parking attendants, or babysitters for such community events.

Promoting Learning Across the Curriculum

Ann Henderson and Karen Mapp (2002) concluded, from their meta-analysis of the research, how important the role is that parents play in helping students academically achieve. However, classroom teachers can be either stepping-stones or stumbling blocks to meaningful parent involvement. When teachers offer opportunities to parents to become involved in their child's education, they are facilitating a partnership with parents. Conversely, when teachers do not offer specific strategies to parents or are too territorial, cooperation is brought to a halt. Educating students is a shared responsibility; therefore it is essential that educators find ways to involve parents in the delivery of programs and services to students.

Partnerships not only create stronger parenting skills and safer school environments but also promote community service and improve student academic performance. Students whose parents are involved (income or background are not variables) are more likely to earn higher grades and test scores and to enroll in higher level programs than students with parents who are not involved. These students are more likely to pass their classes. Not only do they attend school regularly, but they also have better social skills, show improved behavior, and adapt well to school. Schools with family partnerships are more successful in sustaining connections that are aimed at improving student achievement.

IDEAS TO USE

110 Recognize student accomplishments in the community.

Survey the parents and the business community to determine if students have accomplished something that would be appropriate to recognize at the school. Accomplishments in the field of athletics, the fine arts, or community service are among those appropriate to recognize.

111 Promote family literacy through book fairs.

This is an obvious strategy that aligns district, school, classroom, and parent goals. The best way to start this process is to contact publishers or local bookstores. Coordinate the event with the school librarian and contact any local authors to see if they will add their expertise to enrich the event. Adding authors and book signings to the fair increases interest, and therefore attendance. Schedule the fair after school. (My suggestion would be right at dismissal time, as many families pick up their children.) This would also be a good opportunity for teacher librarians to add family volunteers to their roster.

112 Promote family literacy through family nights.

Elementary schools could stage a series of family nights emphasizing a different subject each night. Focus on core subjects such as reading, mathematics, social studies, science, as well as technology. This can be done in family groupings so that parents can bring all their children on one evening.

For example, the reading night could start by having teachers model a read aloud, discussing the benefits of reading together and having members of the family doing shared reading.

If you can add some refreshments to these evenings through a potluck or school snacks, so much the better.

113 Promote student literacy through an annual competition.

Design your own annual competition to select the best books for either the class or library. Have students take part in the annual Best Book Awards competition that starts in the classroom and is celebrated at the school level. Have students read a series of books selected by the staff, and have students vote for the best book. Short summaries/critiques of the book can be submitted by the students. Grade 1 students can submit pictures, right up to Grade 12 students, who can offer a substantive critique.

Involve the advisory council in designing a school assembly, a field trip, or some such special event such a pizza lunch to reward the top ten winners.

114 Promote family literacy through a read-a-thon.

Reward parents reading to their children and children reading to their parents through a read-a-thon. Establish a specific timeline. Start on a Monday and finish on a Monday. Set goals as a class for evening and weekend reading (ranging from 200 minutes for the primary students to 400 minutes for the intermediate students during a three-week stretch). Parents read to or read with their child during this time. Have teachers and students prepare a progress report each Monday morning. Post a chart in the main hallway indicating the progress each class has made toward reaching their goal. Count the progress through number of minutes read. Give all the parents and students who reach their reading goal by the end of the established time a certificate. Celebrating such events through a school assembly highlights the importance of the activity.

115 Spring into fitness.

Involve parents in working with students on increased physical fitness. Have students develop aerobic, rope skipping, or dance routines to be showcased at a school assembly. Focus on an overall healthy lifestyle by planning a potluck featuring nutritionally sound fare.

116 Help form book discussion groups.

Initiate this activity in the classroom as part of the focus on literacy. You can conduct the book club through an online discussion link or in person. Open the membership to students, parents, and the community at large. Intergenerational discussion provides students with adult perspectives other than those of their teachers and parents. It also serves to keep community members in touch with young people. Ask the advisory council to purchase a "book of the month" for the school library based on the selection made by the book group.

117 Implement a schoolwide conservation plan.

As part of the science curriculum, work with parent volunteers to develop a recycle plan in each classroom. Offer incentives to classrooms to become involved. Have students use utensils and plates from home for school events and lunches instead of using paper plates or polystyrene. Act as a recycling depot for the community. Call the local telephone company and participate in recycling telephone books. In addition to the positive effect on the environment, sponsoring paper and aluminum drives has the added benefit of raising money for the school.

118 Visit parents' job sites on field trips.

Government offices, retail stores, hospitals, factories, universities, farms, banks, schools, and nursing homes are just some examples of trips that align well with curriculum. Have the parent conduct the tour when possible.

119 Incorporate elements of the community into the curriculum.

If a unit on pioneers is being taught, then elicit cooperation from the city or municipal office in allowing students to participate in a mock activity of filing for sections of land like original homesteaders. Or invite longtime community members to speak to students about the community's history.

120 Incorporate curriculum support.

Teachers have an opportunity to involve family members as volunteers to academically support students. Under the direction of teachers, volunteers can listen to students read, support small group instruction, read to students, or support hands-on activities. It simply requires planning and direction. Once teachers have had a successful program involving volunteers, they will be reluctant to give up the additional support.

Building Character

R alph Waldo Emerson (1837) once said that "character is higher than intellect." Parents and schools are charged with cultivating the intellect as well as building character. By using a parent and school partnership to provide opportunities for students to realize that their actions can influence others and in turn have an influence on the world, both character and intellect are strengthened.

Simple projects undertaken by teachers and students can promote social responsibility by having students care for the larger community. These activities provide students with opportunities to make charitable and meaningful contributions.

IDEAS TO USE

121 Sponsor a child from a developing country through groups such as UNICEF or the Red Cross.

Make sure the funds needed for the sponsorship come from student fundraising efforts. Teach the students about where their child lives. Have classes study the culture, economics, and geography of their child's homeland. Remember that this needs to be an ongoing project that encompasses twelve months of the year. The school, as an organization, adopts children and carries the responsibility for continued funding over a period of time. Be clear about the time commitment and financial responsibility that are made when the child is adopted.

122 Adopt a sister school.

Have the school collaborate with a school in a different part of the town, state, province, or county to broaden understanding. Select a school in a different setting. A school in a big city could partner with a school in a rural area, for example. Initial connections can be made teacher to teacher via the Internet. Plan visits, both day trips and overnighters, to expand the connections.

123 Provide community service.

Develop student-mentoring programs at your school to build interpersonal connections among and between students.

Mentors can provide academic, social, or emotional support.

Plant tulip bulbs on the school grounds (or at a local senior home) to commemorate Remembrance Day, Veteran's Day, or some other important event.

The advisory council can support community service financially by collecting warm clothing, blankets, and sleeping bags for the homeless during the winter. Ask a local charity to help with distribution.

124 Connect at a conference.

Have students, parents, grandparents, and teachers plan a full day conference to consider current issues such as the environment, effective communication, or the impact of technology. Select themes that can be offered to all delegates at the conference. Intersperse lectures and workshops with social activities such as a box lunch, family dance, or craft fair.

Talking Person to Person

P arent-teacher conferences are often stressful for students, parents, and teachers alike. Prepare parents and students for the experience to ensure that it is positive for all parties concerned. Let students be active partners in planning for the conference. Remember that parents have a right and a responsibility to be involved in their child's education. Expect parents to provide insights, seek clarification, and pose questions. Be open and honest.

IDEAS TO USE

125 Host student-led conferences.

Invite parents to spend time with their children to learn about their child's progress. Have the students lead the conference while the teacher acts as facilitator. This places the students in the position of presenting their portfolio to their parent with the support of the teacher. Properly planned and delivered, these conferences offer a rich experience for both the student and the parent.

126 Prepare the student for the conference.

Have the student help prepare for the conference either by filling out a form or by having a fellow student interview him or her.

In either case, the student should answer the following questions:

- Do you enjoy school? Why or why not?
- What do you do best in school?
- Where do you want to improve?
- What work of yours would you like your parents to see?
- What is the best thing that has happened to you at school in the last year?
- Where have you improved the most?
- What will you do to help achieve your goals?
- How can your parents help you to succeed in school?

127 Other ways to communicate.

Host Before-School Meetings

Invite parents to meet with teachers before school starts. This will lay the foundation for positive communication for the entire year.

Develop Parent Progress Reports

If the system is not already in place in the school, solicit regular feedback from students and parents. Use a report to give feedback to parents concerning their role in supporting the school and their child's education. Send this informal report home twice a year and include feedback related to attendance, homework, signed papers, and school uniforms (if applicable).

128 Keep parents informed, between report card and conference times, about the curriculum covered.

Discuss the instructional and assessment strategies used. Put as much as possible into written form (e.g., class newsletters, bulletins, and class Web site).

129 Consider holding conferences in other locations.

Going to places other than the school, such as the student's home, a local restaurant, or the community library, is a unique "out of the box" way of indicating to the parents and families that there is flexibility in the system. Many parents have a low comfort level in the class setting because of their own experience with the system.

Use conference time as an opportunity to ask how parents feel about the school and its programs. Have a volunteer sign-up sheet handy. The parent-teacher conference should be viewed as a communication opportunity from both the parent's and the teacher's point of view.

Fundraising

Fundraising will always be a major opportunity to involve parents. It is important, however, that fundraising not be the only way in which parents are asked to volunteer their time. While it is a necessary function, it is only one of many roles in the parent-school partnership.

When parental help in raising funds is sought, be specific about what the funds will support. Funds collected by or through the help of parents and students help bridge the gap created by budget shortfalls and are increasingly important to the successful operation of many schools. Athletics, the arts, and enrichment programs often could only be run with moneys received through fundraisers.

Ideas to Use

130 Offer desktop publishing/secretarial support services.

Have business education students offer their services to small businesses. Work could be done through a small business set up by students, and the products could be exchanged via e-mail as well as in person.

131 Create a cookbook for children.

This could be the result of a classroom writing project that is facilitated and supported by parent volunteers who do desktop publishing of the book.

Have students pick their favorite dish and bring the recipe to the classroom.

132 Feature graduating seniors in the school newsletter using their baby pictures.

Sell these "congratulatory" photo ads to parents who can write the accompanying text. Ask the graduates to add their comments. These can be posted on a Web site, used for writing projects, or sold to fellow graduates as a fundraiser for safe graduation celebrations.

133 Invite families to decorate a gingerbread house in their own unique way.

In addition to involving families, ask local celebrities such as teachers, the mayor, or the police chief to each decorate a house. Offer prizes for the most creative. Auction or raffle the gingerbread houses at holiday time.

134 Have students participate in a work-a-thon.

This will not only raise funds but also provide a much need community service. Offer services, such as window washing, backyard cleanup, and painting, at a minimal charge. Be sure that the senior citizens in your community have first access to student services.

135 Host a fashion show.

Work with local dress shops, and have practical arts students model the clothes they made along with the ones from the retail shops. As part of the event, provide an opportunity for participants to try on and purchase the clothing with the school receiving a percentage of the resulting sales.

PART 4

Venturing Beyond the Bake Sale

P arents must be involved beyond the traditional roles of "room mother" and fundraising chairperson. In order to feel valued and involved, parents or caregivers must be involved in the making and implementation of school policy. Parents who are involved in policy making remain involved throughout the policy implementation and evaluation processes.

Joyce Epstein (as cited in Davis, 2000) stated that there are six ways to promote meaningful parent involvement:

1. Design effective forms of school-to-home and home-to-school communication about school programs and children's progress;

2. Help all families establish home environments to support children as students;

3. Recruit and organize parent help and support;

4. Provide information and ideas to families about how to help students at home with homework and other curriculum-related activities, decisions, and planning;

5. Include parents in school decisions, developing parent leaders and representatives; and

6. Identify and integrate resources and services from the community to strengthen school programs, family practices, and student learning and development. (p. 1)

The success of public education is dependent upon public support. Consequently, educators must be responsive to students, parents, and the community at large in order to garner and sustain said support. Parents do not want to run schools, but they do want more shared responsibility in decision making. If the operational norms of a district are based on the principles of collaboration, consultation, and advice, then appropriate involvement of all partners is ensured.

Ann Henderson and Karen Mapp (2002) observed:

Schools that succeed in engaging families from very diverse backgrounds share three key practices. They focus on building trusting, collaborative relationships, among teachers, families and community members, recognize, respect and address family's needs, as well as cultural and class differences, and embrace a philosophy of partnership where power and responsibility are shared. (p. 13)

Establishing Connections

When a group of individuals (staff and parents) that do not know each other come together for meetings, structure ways to have them interact that are not threatening. When a person is put at ease and welcomed as part of a group, that person will contribute more.

At the beginning of a meeting, put participants at ease by having them spend a few minutes getting to know each other. Educators are constantly in meetings, but not all parents are. Therefore be sensitive to the fact that parents may feel apprehensive about participating as part of a group.

IDEAS TO USE

136 Back to back.

Have participants partner with someone in the room they do not know. Provide each person with a sheet of paper and a pen. Have them spend a few minutes talking about why they happen to be at the meeting and what their perceived role is there. After a couple of minutes, have them sit back to back and answer the following questions about their respective partners:

- How tall is the person?
- What color are his or her eyes?
- What jewelry does the person have on?
- Does the person wear glasses?
- What is the person wearing?

Have them turn around and check their memories. Use this as an opener to talk about first impressions, memories, and the way they communicated when they met. Have them debrief and use the exercise as a platform to talk about perceptions and communication.

137 Take three.

Ask participants to introduce themselves to someone with whom they are not acquainted in the room using only three items found on their person. For example, a child's photograph, a scarf, and a briefcase. If a person does not have three items, they may use imagined items.

138 Play twenty questions.

Have persons pair up with individuals they do not know. Tell them they must be prepared to introduce the person to the group by discerning the following information:

- The person's name
- Where the person lives
- Two or three interesting facts about the person

The interviewers are limited to asking only twenty questions of their subject, and their subject may respond to the questions only with a yes or no answer.

After they have each had the opportunity to ask the twenty questions, they introduce each other to the group using the information they obtained from the yes/no responses.

Cross-Fertilizing Ideas

Most parents have a vision of what they want for their children's education; however, they need the opportunity to effectively communicate that vision. Correspondingly, teachers and administrators need to share their vision of the optimum teaching and learning situation. Therefore it is important to provide an opportunity for both to discuss what constitutes an effective learning environment for students. To make the discussion effective, demonstrate that parent opinions are valued by including them in the process of setting annual goals. Structure ways to invite parent input and to respond to their ideas, or parents will probably stop being involved.

Consider the following. Another common reason for lack of parental involvement may be the perceptions families hold about the school. Gwen Rudney (2005) observed:

> Why don't parents come to school? There may be financial and logistical problems. Are schedules too rigid? Is transportation a problem? Perhaps the parents distrust or dislike schools. How were they treated as a student? How well do the teachers and administrators communicate? There may be a language barrier not only for non-English speakers, but also non-jargon speakers. For those who don't understand educational jargon, it may be confusing or intimidating. For those who do understand it, it may be irritating. (p. 85)

Teamwork necessitates that persons be thoughtful and considerate of others. Individuals working effectively together need a sense that they are valued as individuals as well as members of the team. When they feel valued, they are more willing to become interdependent with other members of a team.

Use the following strategies at workshops, advisory council meetings, and parent education sessions. Wisdom is not the prerogative of the few, and the school will benefit from collective thinking. Each of the following should be implemented for the purpose of making parent participation easy.

IDEAS TO USE

139 Begin with the abstract.

Divide parents into groups, and have each group design an advertisement for an ideal school. With group work, the most effective size is six members. It is best to have representatives of different roles in the group (parents, teachers, support staff, administrators). If you are in a middle or secondary school, include the students.

Tell the groups that the ad will be placed in the local newspaper, and the only way the school will enroll students will be through responses to this ad. Therefore the ad needs to list the positive attributes that would attract students and parents. Share the ads from the different groups. Identify the commonalities among the ads. The activity promotes discussion of common beliefs about education and can be a springboard for goal setting.

140 Hats off to good ideas.

Post large pieces of chart paper around the room. At the top of each sheet write a general heading related to one of the topics on which you want input. (The same heading can be repeated a number of times.) Divide each sheet into two columns. On the left side, draw a black hat, and on the right side draw a yellow hat. Ask parent and staff participants to write their concerns, issues, and challenges beneath the black hat. Strengths, compliments, and suggestions should go beneath the yellow hat. Don't have more than three or four group members working at one time on a sheet. Gauge the number of sheets you put up according to the number of participants. Limit discussion to five topics at any one meeting.

141 Fill in the blanks.

Have parents complete the following sentences at a meeting, through a class or school newsletter, by a telephone survey, or through the school Web site. Ask the same questions at least twice a year. Be sure the respondents understand that the intent of the survey is to improve the quality of education offered students. Personnel issues should be dealt with on an individual basis.

It would also be interesting for students in middle or secondary school to respond to the questions or interview their parents using the questions.

- The school is best known for . . .
- If I had a magic wand, I would change the school by . . .
- I could be involved in the school in the following manner . . .
- The best way of communicating with me as a parent/ student is . . .

142 Attach a Beefs and Bouquets form to both the paper and the electronic newsletter.

Beefs and Bouquets is an open-ended form that allows the reader to make comments. "Beefs" are areas of concern that the reader wants the school to be informed of, and "Bouquets" represent positive feedback related to the strengths. The authors of the newsletter could target this section for feedback on a particular item. For example, if a new method of communicating with parents is in place, the school could target the Beefs and Bouquets section to receiving input on that particular topic. Be prepared to deal with the criticisms as well as the compliments. Complete the advice cycle by responding to those that signs their comments. (See the Advice Cycle diagram, below.) The newsletter on the Web site should include the same section.

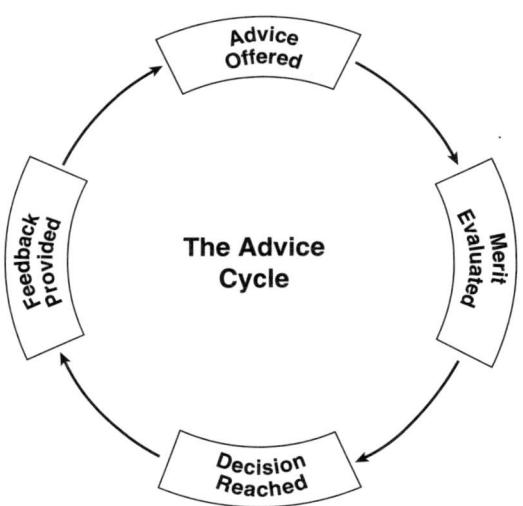

143 Monitor how inviting it is to be a member of the school community.

A school community (parents, staff, and students) should discuss the following questions:

- How do staff and students greet visitors?
- How are new staff, students, and parents welcomed into the school community?
- Is there a welcoming plan in place, or does it just happen by chance?

- Are students, parents, and/or staff asked when they are leaving how they felt about the school as a community?
- Are they asked what they most enjoyed and what they would change?
- Are the contributions of each parent group acknowledged equitably?

144 Toe the line.

This particular exercise is useful in randomly organizing groups and ensures a cross-section of thinking about a particular topic. You may wish to begin the exercise by having them discuss a fun topic such as the pros of smart cars (+ side) And the cons of smart cars (– side).

Arrange two lines of chairs facing each other, directly across from one another. As parents arrive, hand them a piece of paper with either a plus sign (+) or a minus sign (–). All persons with minus signs sit on one side, and all persons with plus signs sit on the other. There needs to be a minimum of ten persons to do this exercise effectively. The person with the plus sign has to present the benefits of a topic to the person sitting across from him or her (toeing the other side of the line) while the person with the minus sign has to listen quietly. Each person then moves three seats to the right and the exercise is repeated, but this time the plus sign presents the cons and the minus sign states the pros. Do this no more than three times. Then have the participants break up into groups of four (two plus signs and two minus signs) and develop a position statement on the topic at hand.

145 Follow the bouncing ball.

The activity needs to be done with a group of persons who work together. In addition, it would be a good activity for an advisory council meeting just prior to a holiday. The chairperson of the meeting hands out a sheet of paper to each participant. The handout asks for information based on six personal questions.

- What is your favorite beverage?
- What is your favorite color?
- What is your favorite activity when you have free time?
- What is your favorite television show?
- What is your favorite holiday spot?
- What is your favorite food?

Participants write their names on the paper. Then have everyone stand in a circle and scrunch the sheet with his or her answers on it into a ball and toss it. Everyone keeps picking up the papers and tossing them until the chairperson tells them to stop. Each person picks up a "scrunched ball" and opens it.

Tell participants to note the person's name and the information on the sheet and keep it a secret. Their responsibility is to do something nice for that person by a specific time. If people pick up their own sheet, the chairperson needs to organize an exchange.

146 Conduct a human treasure hunt.

With a little revision, the same questions asked in number 145 can be used. Hand out the following questions to persons as they walk in the door and ask them to search for persons whose

- favorite beverage is lemonade.
- favorite color is blue.
- favorite activity is hiking.
- favorite TV show is *Survivor.*
- favorite holiday spot is in Mexico.
- favorite food is pizza.

Have them sign the sheet and hand it in when they have completed it. Draw two or three names and award small prizes (a school pen, box of candy, or a plant).

147 Color coordinate the discussion.

Post chart paper with a different band of color (red, yellow, green, and blue) at each corner of the room before the meeting begins. Assign a discussion topic to each color. As parents enter the room, hand them a colored piece of paper (red, yellow, green, or blue). Assign a discussion topic to each color. Individuals gather at the appropriate chart and discuss the topic for a maximum of ten minutes. Plan for anywhere from forty to sixty minutes for this activity, depending on the number of charts the groups are asked to visit. Within each of the color groups, ask the individual wearing the most of that particular color to report three key insights. Each color group must decide what is to be reported to the group as a whole. The facilitator charts the insights on the overhead. The group then moves to another color/topic and repeats the activity. If there is time during the session, it is better to have groups go to all charts so they feel they have had input on all issues. Compile the insights as feedback and circulate to those who were in attendance.

148 Never-ending chain.

A fun way of generating ideas is to form groups of six and start the brainstorming by asking parents to suggest ideas. For example, begin with the topic of how the school can support the family. The first parent states a method, the second parent adds to it, as does the third, and so on. After the sixth person has added his or her method, the group charts the idea. The second parent starts with the next idea, the next adds to it, and so on. Do this until each person has initiated an idea.

Fostering Effective Advisory Councils

Advisory councils are a formal group involved in school governance. The council should be involved in studying school issues, planning for improvements, and fostering positive school and community relationships. The key focus is to improve the quality of school life. Every school has an advisory council that includes parent representation. The mandates or names may change from place to place, but societal expectations relating to school accountability remain the same.

An effective advisory council will improve the trust, morale, and cohesion of the school community. The council should have both continuity and turnover in its membership, have enough members to serve the needs of the school community, and meet with appropriate frequency.

IDEAS TO USE

149 Involve those affected by decisions.

For the most part, educators believe in the positive implications of parent involvement. Most educators are comfortable with parents being involved and supportive of their child's achievement as well as comfortable with parents as volunteers in school. It is when parents want to become involved in decision making that parent involvement becomes a contentious issue. Educators are protective of their professional domain, while parents are demanding greater accountability and involvement. Achieving a balance between the partners' needs is the key to success.

Decisions that were once considered to be the domain of the educator are now a part of a shared governance mandate. Parents are very much a part of the new accountability movement, which influences the delivery of educational programs and services. Educators and parents need to learn to govern together, because doing so will inevitably improve the quality of decisions.

150 Develop district-operating principles.

Clarify decision-making procedures that support and encourage parents' involvement in decision making, and determine who is going to be responsible for what actions. Establish procedures that ensure that those affected by the decisions have an opportunity to be involved in the decision-making process.

Policies and procedures should not be set without completely analyzing the implications. Complete the advice cycle. (See the Advice Cycle diagram.)

151 Ensure clear and timely agendas for meetings.

List the speaker and time expected to cover the topic. Indicate whether the topic is limited or open for discussion. Provide opportunities for input into the agenda; perhaps at the end of each meeting, begin setting the agenda for the next. Set a deadline of three days prior to the meeting for additions to the agenda.

Make agendas for upcoming meetings available in advance. A good idea would be to e-mail meeting agendas several days in advance.

Include the agenda on the district and school Web sites or issue as a press release to the media.

152 Expand the membership of the council.

Include representatives from the community at large. Seek out members from business, industry, social service agencies, faith-based organizations, and local government and invite them to serve.

153 Annually revisit the purpose, belief statements, and mission statement of your advisory council.

This will ensure that it reflects the perspective of all the partner groups annually. It is important that advisory council members clearly understand their mandate. The clearly defined mandate needs to be articulated and shared not only with staff and parents but also with other social service agencies and the community at large.

154 Allow all members of the school community direct input into the creation of the district's and school's mission statements.

Know the "voices" that should be represented in the partnership. Consider representatives of the business council, colleges, universities, students, parent groups, teachers, and administrators. Consider who should be there, and invite them to be part of the group.

It is important to have school advisory councils and other parent groups define their missions and beliefs in this way. Creating a mission statement is the first step toward setting goals because the overall focus of an organization is then well defined. When representatives of the partner organizations come to the table to set the school and district mission statement, they should understand the foundation of their own operations.

Mission statements then become the filter through which all school decisions must pass.

155 Set annual goals.

Schools all too often exclude parents from the goal-setting process and simply announce what the goals of the school are. The challenge is to meaningfully involve parents in setting school goals. Once accomplished, the combined pool of wisdom will ensure that better decisions are made. Parents will consequently be more supportive of steps taken to reach the goals because they were consulted on the formation of the goals in the first place.

Goals and objectives must be "user-friendly," remembering that the users in many cases will not be trained educators but laypersons. The language as well as the depth and scope of the goals and activities must be realistic. All participants should have equal input into the decision to ensure that it is a product of collective thinking.

156 SOCC it to them.

This activity could be done at an advisory council, a home and school association, or a joint meeting with the staff. List the Strengths, Opportunities, and Change to Consider (or SOCC). After each area is analyzed, regroup the participants and ask them to develop a three-year action plan that includes the following:

- Timeline over the three years with strategies prioritized
- Key person(s) or group heading the campaign
- Budget implications
- Evaluation strategies
- Staff, parent, and student development activities

The activity identifies the major areas of strength and the challenges faced by the school. Things that need to be changed or rethought are put into focus.

Provide *all* parents and staff with an opportunity for input. Include students in the goal-setting process where appropriate.

Debrief meetings (including online discussions and meetings) via e-mail. Allow a day or so for participants to digest the information, and then send in comments.

157 Give advance notice.

Set the schedule of meetings for the whole year. Arrange events and meetings during times when most parents can attend. This may result in having to schedule some during the day and some at night. Vary the day of the week meetings are held. Advertise council meetings prior to the event.

158 Develop a system of communicating the outcomes of meetings.

This could be accomplished via newsletter, resource persons, bulletin boards, and Web sites or by broadcasting a video of the meeting on the community's cable access channel.

159 Clarify the mandate of the council.

Depending on the political setting, the council could be involved in staffing, budget preparations, curricular planning, facilities issues, and program evaluation.

Many types of councils have legislated responsibilities. Ensure that everyone translates those into clear operational guidelines.

160 Ensure council members address the following.

- Current reports about student achievement on provincial and state tests as well as other school assessments
- Up-to-date information about the school and the board
- Ways to consult and communicate with all parents, families, and the community in general
- Ways to provide input on issues and the process to determine how the input was received

161 Gauge the productivity and value of meetings.

Debrief immediately afterward. This could be done verbally or in written form or by e-mail.

Establish operational norms for the meeting, including rules of order and protocol.

Have the council determine whether they wish to develop a handbook and a code of conduct for the council.

162 Establish formal ways that the advisory council and the staff can discuss and provide feedback to each other through joint meetings.

If this isn't feasible, have representatives attend each other's meetings and report back to their respective groups.

In some cases, and depending on your policies and procedures, parent reps could come to portions of the staff meetings and report out and discuss the mandates and activities of the advisory council.

Staff members, besides the school administration, could attend the advisory council meetings on a rotating basis and report out and discuss staff mandates and school programs.

163 Understand district policies and procedures.

Make parents aware of the appropriate procedure for not only evaluating but also providing input to the system. Be sure that staff is trained to react to parent concerns in a positive way. An accepted procedure for addressing parent grievances is to first discuss the issue or concern with the teacher or staff member involved. Then, if not resolved, discuss the situation with the principal. Make the names, office telephone numbers, and e-mail addresses of district personnel available to parents.

164 Perform an ABC evaluation at a parent and/or staff meeting.

Ask participants to finish the following sentences:

A. An action(s) that should be taken as a result of this meeting is . . .
B. The best part of the meeting was . . .
C. Concerns I have are . . .

Developing Parent Capacity

O ften educators use technical or professional jargon that functionally creates barriers to parent understanding of the educational system. Parents must be afforded avenues of inquiry into the current practices, research, and terminology specific to education. To this end, effort and priority must be given to the very real need for parent development so that parents can fully participate in the education of their children.

Well-informed and educated parents make the best partners. Cultivate every opportunity to inform and educate parents. Be sure to offer presentations that are appropriate to a variety of learning styles.

IDEAS TO USE

165 Add a parent development strand to district staff development inservices.

If the teaching staff is learning about proposed curriculum changes and teaching strategies, then host parallel sessions for parents. Promote the parent strand through school information methods. Ask parents to register either at their school or online to ensure that proper accommodations can be provided.

166 Make parent development a regular part of advisory council meetings.

Designate a member of the advisory council to implement parent education programs. Open council meetings with a guest speaker or close them with an open forum on an education topic. Have faculty or administrative staff act as resource speakers or discussion facilitators.

167 Form a district partners planning group that offers inservices on a variety of topics.

Plan four sessions per year on a districtwide basis. Address topics such as literacy, student discipline, budgeting, and vandalism.

168 Establish a parent library.

Allow parents access to the professional resource materials usually reserved for teachers. Collect print as well as video and audio resources. Include materials on curriculum change, instructional strategies, and the latest research findings. Invite parents to come in and browse and borrow.

Provide links on the Web site for the parent library consisting of Internet links to articles and other educational resources.

169 Host special sessions for parents and other family members.

Topics could include the following:

- How to help your child with homework
- The holistic development of the child
- Emergency preparedness
- Basic fire safety
- Study skills
- Drug and alcohol awareness

Be sure that the sessions are held when and where it is most convenient for the target audience, the parents.

In addition, write up this information as a handout, Power Point, or word processing document and send it via e-mail as a topic of the month. In case recipients do not have access to the programs used, include it as text in an e-mail message.

170 Invite parents to drop in at the school on their way home from work to engage in some friendly conversation.

Establish a routine and notify parents of what days administrators, school counselors, a specific grade level's group of teachers, or advisory council members will be available to chat. If the school has a track, invite the community to use the shower facilities after their respective daily runs.

171 Plan "Advocates for Education" seminars.

For example, if there is major change occurring in the district (decline or growth in student enrollment, reorganization of school models, new electives, and boundary changes), train teams of speakers to present to the community. Invite parents to be part of the team, and train them along with educators.

172 Offer an annual parent conference through the district partnership committee or district advisory council.

Schedule it for a Saturday between nine o'clock in the morning and two o'clock in the afternoon for the best chance at full participation. Charge a minimal fee to ensure attendance. Choose a topic that appeals to a variety of interests. Allow online registration. Advertise in the school and district newsletters and Web sites. Take advantage of free community announcements provided by local radio and cable stations.

District Initiatives: Setting the Example

District beliefs and operational principles must not only set policy for the schools in the district but must also set an example. Policy needs to center around offering sound educational programs and services to students in collaboration and consultation with parents.

Considering that all states have established academic content standards for public school students and are in the process of aligning curricula, instruction, assessment, and reporting, the education of parents and community members (as well as students, teachers, and administrators) is a complex and important task (Riggins-Newby, 2004).

Parental involvement is the cornerstone of any educational system. It must be made a priority in the district. Consequently, school-based practices will align with that of the district. Districts must model the concept that governance of a district is a community responsibility.

IDEAS TO USE

173 Develop an annual district survey.

Use the first annual results as benchmarks to set standards for improvement. Use the district Web site, school Web sites, local media, and regular mail to distribute the survey.

Share the results of the survey in the same public fashion.

174 Establish a standing district committee.

Create a district committee whose mandate it is to enhance and improve the quality of community relations.

Ensure that all the partner groups are represented on the committee.

Articulate the board's vision as it relates to involving families and share it on the district Web site.

Define district expectations regarding parent involvement to include the influence parents have in school and district decision making.

Provide a policy that incorporates the role of school advisory councils in policy development.

Clarify the policies around fundraising at the district and school levels.

Allocate funds annually to support advisory councils.

175 As a district, expect that schools will have school councils with parent representatives.

This has become a legislated mandate; the role of the district is to ensure that the parameters are met from both an educational and a legal perspective. Many of us have experienced groups who are sabotaged by a belief system that they really should not exist. The beliefs of the educators will determine the success of councils fulfilling their shared governance role.

176 Hold school board meetings and district forums in sites other than the board office.

Use community centers, faith-based sites, local schools, and city chambers. The willingness to be available to the public in a variety of venues adds credence to the stated belief that the school board values public input.

Resources

Web Sites Focusing on
Involving Families

U sing all the popular browsers, I identified more than 17,300,000 different Web sites using the key words "Involving Families in Education." I reviewed a significant number of the sites, paying special attention to the level of relevancy identified by the browser. Those that best spoke to the issue of involving families at all levels appear here.

Each site is listed with its relevant Internet address. The Web protocol for each site is http://. In addition to domain names (as in the fictitious example www.involvingparents .com), subdirectory information is provided so that the user can obtain specific data. Information stored at a site's subdirectory is separated from the domain name by a slash (as is the case with www.involvingparents.com/resources).

BC Confederation of Parent Advisory Councils

www.bccpac.bc.ca

This organization is the voice of the provincial parent advisory councils and as such is the "collective voice of parents for the best possible public education of all children in British Columbia." Its purpose is to improve public education through the support of parents and students. It focuses on proactively advancing public education by participating in every level of education (from site based to provincial levels).

The site provides insightful information for projects such as advocacy and understands the fundamental concept that parents are an integral part of the education system.

This is an interesting educational source for educators as well as parents and the community.

Communities in Schools

www.cisnet.org

Communities in Schools, a not-for-profit organization previously called Cities in Schools. Based in Alexandria, Virginia, the organization and its Web site offers down-to-earth ideas and conducts partnership classes for interested organizations. Whether or not Communities in Schools has a regional office in your area, they can provide help and direction to your programs.

Education Commission of the States

www.ecs.org

Provides current news clips and links to what is taking place in education. It includes "background and basic information about an issue, links to more information on the ECS Web site, and places and people to contact if you need still more." The stated purpose is to help state leaders form educational policy.

Education World: The Educator's Best Friend

www.education-world.com

This well-designed site is an extensive resource for parents and teachers. It deals with school issues ranging from teacher retention to legislation and assessment as well as offering excellent, well-researched archived articles. The site is organized into topics of interest as well as roles and responsibilities.

Involving Hispanic Parents in Their Children's Education

www.gse.harvard.edu/hfrp/projects/ fine/resources/research/golan.html

This site is called Family Involvement: Promoting Involvement of Recent Immigrant Families in Their Children's Education. This site provides a research-based article that discusses how to involve Hispanic parents in the education of their children. It presents a training model that was developed by both educators and members of the Hispanic community.

This site, offered by the Harvard Family Research Project, has links to extensive research on the topic of family involvement. A site well worth exploring for both educators and parents.

Middle Web

www.middleweb.com

A site devoted to educational reform at the middle school level. Components of this reform include strategies for involving parents in their child's education.

National Center for Educational Statistics

www.nces.ed.gov/

This site reports findings from the National Center for Educational Statistics. It is the primary organization for the U.S. federal government in collecting and analyzing educational data for the country.

It provides insightful information for educators as well as families. Well worth browsing through to gain a more global understanding of education.

National Coalition for Parent Involvement in Education

www.ncpie.org/

The organization was founded in 1980, and their mission is "to advocate the involvement of parents and families in their children's education, and to foster relationships between home, school, and community to enhance the education of our nation's young people."

Provides current research from experts in the field of parent involvement. The intended audience is parents, administrators, and teachers. Excellent site with an extensive list of resources as well as legislative information.

Schoolnotes.com

www.schoolnotes.com/

This site allows educators to post class and school information as well as homework. It is a free community service with a stated purpose of connecting teachers with families by allowing them to post up-to-date information. The site is user friendly and has free registration. Teachers can create notes and families can view them.

Southwest Educational Development Laboratory (SEDL)

www.sedl.org/pubs/sedl-letter/

This monthly newsletter reports on current issues related to teaching and learning, with a special emphasis on student achievement. The findings cover best practices from local and national perspectives.

The purpose of this private, not-for-profit corporation is to "work with educators, parents, community members, and policymakers to build, find and use strategies and tools addressing educational problems."

Excellent site for practitioners and the community at large.

Teachers Helping Teachers

www.pacificnet.net/~mandel/

A site featured in *Education Week* and *Teacher Magazine* has very current and interesting ideas for teachers written by teachers. The teacher chat board is a good place to network and share ideas with other professionals about involving parents.

Teachers.net

www.teachers.net

In addition to chat and lesson plans, search this site for ever-changing implementation plans and ideas on how to bring about and use parent involvement.

References

British Columbia Confederation of Parent Advisory Councils. (1998). *BCCPAC advocacy report.* Vancouver: BCCPAC Offices.

Cairncross, F. (2001). *The death of distance: How the communication revolution is changing our lives.* Boston: Harvard Business School Press.

Charles, C. M., & Mertler, C. A. (2002). *Introduction to educational research* (4th ed.). Boston: Allyn & Bacon.

Chen, X., & Chandler, K. (2001). *Efforts by public k-8 schools to involve parents in children's education: Do school and parent reports agree?* [Electronic version]. National Center for Education Statistics: U.S. Department of Education Office of Educational Research. Washington, DC.

Covey, S. (1989). *The seven habits of highly effective people.* New York: Fireside Press.

Davis, D. (2000). Supporting family and community involvement in your school. *North West Regional Educational Laboratory.* Retrieved August 10, 2005, from http://www.nwrel.org/csrdp/family.Parent (Available at http://www.nwrel.org/csrdp/family.pdf)

DuFour, R. (2000, Winter). Community: Data put a face on shared vision. *Journal of Staff Development, 21,* 1.

Emerson, R. W. *The American scholar.* August 31, 1837. An oration before the Phi Beta Kappa Society, at Cambridge University.

Epstein, J. (1995). School/Family/Community partnerships: Caring for the children we share. *Phi Delta Kappan, 76,* 9, 701–712.

Epstein, J. L., Coates, L., Salinas, K. C., Sanders, M. G., & Simon, B. S. (1997). *School, family, and community partnerships: Your handbook for action.* Thousand Oaks, CA: Corwin Press.

Henderson, A., & Mapp, K. (2002). *A new wave of evidence: The impact of school, family and community connections on student achievement. Annual synthesis.* [Electronic version]. National Center for

Family and Community Connections with Schools: Southwest Educational Development Laboratory. U.S. Department of Education.

Huffman, J. B., & Hipp, K. K. (2003). *Reculturing schools as professional learning communities.* Toronto: Scarecrow Education.

Lawrence-Lightfoot, S. (2003, Fall). Questions and answers. *Fine Forum e-Newsletter.* Retrieved August 12, 2005, from www.gse.harvard .edu/hfrp/projects/fine/fineforum/forum7/questions.html

McEwan, E. (2003). *10 traits of highly effective principals: From good to great performance.* Thousand Oaks, CA: Corwin Press.

McLeod, B. (1996). *School reform & student diversity: Exemplary schooling for language minority students.* NCRCDSLL Publications. Retrieved January 26, 2006, from www.ncela.gwu.edu/pubs/ resource/schref.htm

Miedel, W. T., & Reynolds, A. J. (1999). Parent involvement in early intervention for disadvantaged children: Does it matter? *Journal of School Psychology, 37,* 4, 379–402.

National PTA. (2005). Don't talk to me, my friends are watching. *Family Education.* Retrieved August 12, 2005, from www .familyeducation.com/article/0,1120,1–9730,00.html

North Central Regional Education Laboratory. (2005). Retrieved August 10, 2005, from www.ncrel.org/comm/whatsnew/html

Paige, R. (2002, April). Improving America's high schools. *Community Update.* Washington, DC: U.S. Department of Education.

Pearce, T. (2003). *Leading out loud: Inspiring change through authentic communication.* San Francisco, CA: Jossey-Bass.

Riggins-Newby, C. G. (2004). Developing successful partnership programs. *Principal, 83,* 10–15.

Romo, H. (2002). Celebrating diversity to support student success. *SEDL Letter 14, No. 2, May 2002.* Office of English Language Acquisition, Language Enhancement & Academic Achievement for Limited English Proficient Students. Retrieved August 10, 2005, from www.sedl.org/pubs/sedletter/v14n02/4.html

Rudney, G. (2005). *Every teacher's guide to working with parents.* Thousand Oaks, CA: Corwin Press.

Strait School Board. (2005). *School advisory council handbook.* Retrieved August 10, 2005, from http://lsstrait.ednet.ns.ca/ srsb/SRSBoard.nsf/

Teddlie, C., & Reynolds, D. (2000). Current topics and approaches in school effectiveness research: The contemporary field. In C. Teddlie & D. Reynolds (Eds.), *The international handbook of school effectiveness research* (pp. 160–186). New York: Falmer.

Van Fleet, A. (2005). *Leadership communication: Process.* Module Lectures, 1, 16. Miami, FL: Nova Southeastern University.

Wojciuk, J. (2005). *Benefit communications redesigned for diverse workforce.* Retrieved August 10, 2005, from www.business insurance.com

Index

CORWIN PRESS

The Corwin Press logo—a raven striding across an open book—represents the union of courage and learning. Corwin Press is committed to improving education for all learners by publishing books and other professional development resources for those serving the field of PreK–12 education. By providing practical, hands-on materials, Corwin Press continues to carry out the promise of its motto: **"Helping Educators Do Their Work Better."**